Latin

FOR COMMON ENTRANCE

13+

Revision Guide

N.R.R. Oulton

GALORE PARK

AN HACHETTE UK COMPANY

About the author

Nicholas Oulton taught Latin and Greek for ten years before writing the *So you really want to learn Latin* course and founding Galore Park in 1998. He is also the editor of Latin Prep, Books 1–3, and believes Latin to be the most important subject in the school curriculum.

This book is dedicated to the memory of Herodotus, the manuscript-munching cocker spaniel who never had a chance to get his paws on this one.

Acknowledgements

The publishers would like to thank the Independent Schools Examinations Board for permission to use extracts, both adapted and unadapted, from recent Common Entrance papers. Thanks are also due to Stephen Anderson, Senior Tutor at Winchester College, for his scrupulous work in reading the proofs and suggesting numerous improvements.

Every effort has been made to trace all copyright holders, but if any have been inadvertently overlooked, the Publishers will be pleased to make the necessary arrangements at the first opportunity.

Although every effort has been made to ensure that website addresses are correct at time of going to press, Galore Park cannot be held responsible for the content of any website mentioned in this book. It is sometimes possible to find a relocated web page by typing in the address of the home page for a website in the URL window of your browser.

Hachette UK's policy is to use papers that are natural, renewable and recyclable products and made from wood grown in sustainable forests. The logging and manufacturing processes are expected to conform to the environmental regulations of the country of origin.

Orders: **Teachers** please contact Bookpoint Ltd, 130 Park Drive, Milton Park, Abingdon, Oxon OX14 4SE. Telephone: (44) 01235 400555. Email primary@bookpoint.co.uk. Lines are open from 9 a.m. to 5 p.m., Monday to Saturday, with a 24-hour message answering service.

Parents, Tutors please call: 020 3122 6405 (Monday to Friday, 9:30 a.m. to 4.30 p.m.). Email: parentenquiries@galorepark.co.uk

Visit our website at www.galorepark.co.uk for details of other revision guides for Common Entrance, examination papers and Galore Park publications.

ISBN: 978 1 4718 5344 9

© N.R.R. Oulton 2015

First published in 2015 by

Galore Park Publishing Ltd,

An Hachette UK Company

Carmelite House

50 Victoria Embankment

London EC4Y 0DZ

www.galorepark.co.uk

Impression number   10 9 8 7 6 5 4

Year   2019 2018

Illustration of a roman soldier on p92 by Tony Randell. All other illustrations by Aptara, Inc.

Typeset in India

Printed in India

A catalogue record for this title is available from the British Library.

Contents

Introduction	vi
The syllabus and your exams	vi
Tips on revising	vii

Level 1   1

Chapter 1   3

1.1 Verbs: present tense	3
1.2 Present infinitive	4
1.3 Nouns	5
1.4 Nouns: 1st declension	5
1.5 Nouns: 2nd declension	6
1.6 Subjects and objects	6
1.7 Nouns like **puer** and **magister**	8
1.8 Using all the cases	8

Chapter 2   11

2.1 Adjectives: **bonus**	11
2.2 Agreement of adjectives	11
2.3 Adjectives in –**er**	12
2.4 The verb **sum** = 'to be'	12
2.5 **sum** + complement	12
2.6 Prepositions	13
2.7 Imperatives	14

Chapter 3   17

3.1 Verbs: the imperfect tense	17
3.2 Imperfect of **sum**	18
3.3 Adverbs	18
3.4 Subordinate clauses	19
3.5 Pronouns	19

Chapter 4   22

4.1 The perfect tense	22
4.2 Principal parts	22
4.3 Questions	23
4.4 Golden rules of Latin translation	24
4.5 Numbers	25

Level 2   29

Chapter 5   31

5.1 The future tense	31
5.2 Future of **sum**	31
5.3 3rd declension nouns: **rex**	32
5.4 3rd declension nouns: **nomen**	33
5.5 More on the golden rules of Latin translation	34

Chapter 6   36

6.1 The pluperfect tense   36
6.2 3rd declension adjectives   37
6.3 Other 3rd declension adjectives   38
6.4 Comparison of adjectives   39
6.5 Adjectives in -er and -lis: superlative forms   40
6.6 Irregular comparisons   40

Chapter 7   43

7.1 Pronouns   43
7.2 The reflexive pronoun   44
7.3 More prepositions   45
7.4 Demonstrative pronouns: hic, haec, hoc   45
7.5 Demonstrative pronouns: is, ea, id   45
7.6 Demonstrative pronouns: ille, illa, illud   46
7.7 Prohibitions   47

Chapter 8   49

8.1 More irregular verbs: possum and eo   49
8.2 More questions: nonne and num   50
8.3 Numbers 1–20   51

Level 3   55

Chapter 9   57

9.1 The passive: present tense   57
9.2 The passive: future tense   58
9.3 The passive: imperfect tense   59
9.4 The perfect passive   60
9.5 The pluperfect passive   60

Chapter 10   63

10.1 5th declension nouns: res   63
10.2 Relative pronoun: qui, quae, quod   63
10.3 Relative clauses   64
10.4 More pronouns: ipse   65
10.5 More pronouns: idem   66

Chapter 11   68

11.1 Present participles   68
11.2 Past participle passive (PPP)   69
11.3 Irregular verbs: volo and nolo   70
11.4 Irregular verbs: fero   71
11.5 Expressions of time   71
11.6 Expressions of place   72

Chapter 12   74

12.1 The imperfect subjunctive   74
12.2 Purpose clauses   74
12.3 Indirect command   75
12.4 Numbers 20–100 and 1000   76
12.5 A note on dum = while   76

Non-linguistic studies 79

Chapter 13 Greek mythology 81

13.1 Perseus and Medusa 81
13.2 Jason and the Golden Fleece 81
13.3 Theseus and the Minotaur 82
13.4 The labours of Hercules 82
13.5 The Trojan War 84
13.6 The wanderings of Odysseus 84

Chapter 14 The city of Rome 87

14.1 Romulus and Remus 87
14.2 Horatius 87
14.3 Mucius Scaevola 87
14.4 Cloelia 88
14.5 Coriolanus 88
14.6 Manlius Torquatus 88
14.7 The theatre 89
14.8 The amphitheatre 89
14.9 The circus 89
14.10 Baths 90

Chapter 15 Domestic life 92

15.1 Roman housing 92
15.2 Roman food and meals 93
15.3 Roman clothing 93
15.4 Roman slavery 94
15.5 Life and death 94

Chapter 16 The army and Roman Britain 96

16.1 Army organisation 96
16.2 Army equipment 96
16.3 Army camps 96
16.4 Army tombstones 96
16.5 Julius Caesar in Britain 97
16.6 Claudius, Caratacus and Boudicca 98
16.7 Roman towns and villas 99
16.8 Hadrian's Wall 99

Exam-style question answers 101

Test yourself answers 117

Introduction

This revision guide has been written to help you in preparing for the Common Entrance Examination at 13+, and assumes that you are *revising* this material, not learning it for the first time. It is divided into four main sections, one for each of the three levels in the exam, and a section on the background material, or non-linguistic studies. If you are intending to take Level 1 of the exam, you do not need to revise the Level 2 and Level 3 sections; if you are intending to take Level 2, you do not need to revise the Level 3 section; those taking Level 3 need to revise all sections in this book. The non-linguistic section must be revised for all levels.

Throughout you will find plenty of 'Test yourself' questions that will allow you to check that you have learned a section properly, and 'Exam-style questions' with which you practise the kind of questions that you will see in the exam. There are answers near the back of the book.

At the end of each chapter is a summary of what you should have learned. Make sure that you keep track of what you have and have not covered, and keep practising anything you are unsure of.

The syllabus and your exams

For Common Entrance Latin, you will sit an exam lasting one hour. You will choose one of the three levels, Level 1, Level 2 or Level 3, as agreed with your teacher.

The format of each level is the same, but the material gets harder. In each level, there are four questions worth a total of 75 marks, as follows:

Question 1 (15 marks)

A short passage of Latin will be set, on which you will be asked to answer eight to ten questions, testing your understanding of the passage. You will not be expected to write a translation of the passage, but clearly you need to have translated it in your head, in order to answer the questions.

Question 2 (30 marks)

Another, slightly longer passage will be set, continuing the story from the passage in Question 1. You will be asked to translate this passage, writing your translation on alternate lines.

Question 3 (20 marks)

Another short passage of Latin will be set, continuing the story from the earlier two passages. Questions will be set, testing your knowledge of Latin grammar and how the language works. You will not be asked to translate this passage, but again you will find it difficult to answer the questions unless you have translated it for yourself.

The questions will fall into the following types:

● From the passage give, in Latin, one example of: (an adjective, a preposition followed by the accusative, a noun in the genitive, a verb in the imperfect tense, etc.).

● **erat** (line 2). In which tense is this verb? What is the first person singular of the present tense of this verb?

● **pueros** (line 4). In which case is this noun? Why is this case used?

● **vocaverunt** (line 5). What does this word mean? What is the connection between **vocaverunt** and the English word *vocation*?

- **necat** (line 5) means *he kills*. How would you say in Latin *he was killing* (imperfect tense)?

  And last but not least:

- Using the vocabulary given, translate the following two short sentences into Latin.

Most candidates lose the majority of their marks on Question 3 by falling into the trap of thinking they do not need to translate the passage. They simply guess the answers. To answer a question such as 'in which case is the word **templum** in line 3?', you have to have translated the sentence in which the word **templum** is. Otherwise you will simply be guessing, particularly with a word such as **templum**, which could be any of nominative, vocative or accusative singular.

Question 4 (10 marks)

You will be set eight questions on four areas: Roman domestic life; the city of Rome; the army and Roman Britain; and Greek mythology. Each question will have two parts, part (i) and part (ii). You select **one** question, and answer both parts of it. Examples are given below:

The city of Rome

(c) (i) Tell the story of Cloelia.

   (ii) Which elements of this story would the Romans have found particularly admirable? Explain your answer.

Greek mythology

(h) (i) Tell the story of Odysseus' encounter with the Cyclops.

   (ii) Describe two qualities which Odysseus displayed in this encounter.

These are two of the eight questions that might have been set, labelled (a) to (h). If you had chosen to do the one labelled (c) above, you would have done both part (i) and part (ii) of that question.

Tips on revising

Get the best out of your brain

- Give your brain plenty of oxygen by exercising. You can only revise effectively if you feel fit and well.

- Eat healthy food while you are revising. Your brain works better when you give it good fuel.

- Think positively. Give your brain positive messages so that it will want to study.

- Keep calm. If your brain is stressed, it will not operate effectively.

- Take regular breaks during your study time.

- Get enough sleep. Your brain will carry on sorting out what you have revised while you sleep.

Get the most from your revision

- Don't work for hours without a break. Revise for 20–30 minutes, then take a five-minute break.

- Do good things in your breaks: listen to your favourite music, eat healthy food, drink some water, do some exercise or juggle. Don't read a book, watch TV or play on the computer; it will conflict with what your brain is trying to learn.

- When you go back to your revision, review what you have just learnt.

- Regularly review the material you have learnt.

Get motivated

- Set yourself some goals and promise yourself a treat when the exams are over.

- Make the most of all the expertise and talent available to you at school and at home. If you don't understand something, ask your teacher to explain.

- Get organised. Find a quiet place to revise and make sure you have all the equipment you need.

- Use year and weekly planners to help you organise your time so that you revise all subjects equally. (Available for download from www.galorepark.co.uk)

- Use topic and subject checklists to help you keep on top of what you are revising. (Available for download from www.galorepark.co.uk)

Know what to expect in the exam

- Use past papers to familiarise yourself with the format of the exam.

- Make sure you understand the language examiners use.

Before the exam

- Have all your equipment and pens ready the night before.

- Make sure you are at your best by getting a good night's sleep before the exam.

- Have a good breakfast in the morning.

- Take some water into the exam if you are allowed.

- Think positively and keep calm.

During the exam

- Have a watch on your desk. Work out how much time you need to allocate to each question and try to stick to it.

- Make sure you read and understand the instructions on the front of the exam paper.

- Allow some time at the start to read and consider the questions carefully before writing anything.

- Read every question at least twice. Don't rush into answering before you have a chance to think about it.

LEVEL 1

1.1 Verbs: present tense

Verbs are the key to every sentence – they tell us what is happening.

Latin verbs are made up of a **stem**, which tells us *what* is being done, and an **ending**, which tells us *who* is doing it, and *when*.

Verbs have three persons in the singular and three in the plural:

1st person singular	I
2nd person singular	You (sing.)
3rd person singular	He/she/it
1st person plural	We
2nd person plural	You (pl.)
3rd person plural	They

Verbs have a number of different **tenses**, which relate to when the action is happening. For Level 1, you need to know three of these: present, imperfect and perfect.

Verbs change their endings in different ways to form the different tenses, depending on the **conjugation** to which they belong. There are five regular conjugations to revise and, in the present tense, these go as follows:

1st	2nd	3rd	4th	Mixed
amare = to love	monere = to warn	regere = to rule	audire = to hear	capere = to capture
am-o	mone-o	reg-o	audi-o	cap-io
ama-s	mone-s	reg-is	audi-s	cap-is
ama-t	mone-t	reg-it	audi-t	cap-it
ama-mus	mone-mus	reg-imus	audi-mus	cap-imus
ama-tis	mone-tis	reg-itis	audi-tis	cap-itis
ama-nt	mone-nt	reg-unt	audi-unt	cap-iunt

In many vocabularies, and in Common Entrance exam papers, a verb is usually shown with the number of the conjugation in brackets. Thus **amo** is written **amo** (1), **moneo** is written as **moneo** (2), and so on. Note that the mixed conjugation is shown as (3½).

> The present tense endings of all these verbs are very similar, following the same basic pattern of -o, -s, -t, -mus, -tis, -nt.

When translating a Latin verb into English, always read it backwards! The ending tells you *who*, and the stem tells you *what*:

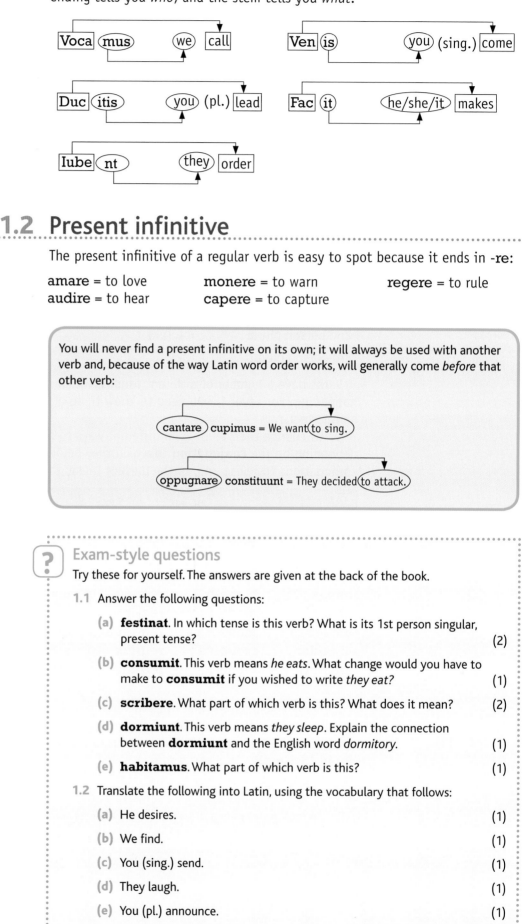

1.2 Present infinitive

The present infinitive of a regular verb is easy to spot because it ends in **-re**:

amare = to love   **monere** = to warn   **regere** = to rule
audire = to hear   **capere** = to capture

You will never find a present infinitive on its own; it will always be used with another verb and, because of the way Latin word order works, will generally come *before* that other verb:

cantare cupimus = We want to sing.

oppugnare constituunt = They decided to attack.

? Exam-style questions

Try these for yourself. The answers are given at the back of the book.

1.1 Answer the following questions:

(a) **festinat**. In which tense is this verb? What is its 1st person singular, present tense? (2)

(b) **consumit**. This verb means *he eats*. What change would you have to make to **consumit** if you wished to write *they eat*? (1)

(c) **scribere**. What part of which verb is this? What does it mean? (2)

(d) **dormiunt**. This verb means *they sleep*. Explain the connection between **dormiunt** and the English word *dormitory*. (1)

(e) **habitamus**. What part of which verb is this? (1)

1.2 Translate the following into Latin, using the vocabulary that follows:

(a) He desires. (1)

(b) We find. (1)

(c) You (sing.) send. (1)

(d) They laugh. (1)

(e) You (pl.) announce. (1)

Total marks: 12

I desire = cupio (3½)	I laugh = rideo (2)
I find = invenio (4)	I announce = nuntio (1)
I send = mitto (3)	

When translating a verb into Latin, be sure to identify which conjugation the Latin verb belongs to (the conjugation number is given in brackets). Then follow the correct endings for that conjugation. If in doubt, refer back to section 1.1.

1.3 Nouns

Nouns in Latin, like verbs, are made up of a stem and an ending. The stem tells us what the noun is, and the ending tells us how it is being used in the sentence.

Nouns may be one of three **genders**: they can be masculine (male), feminine (female) or neuter (neither!).

Nouns have two **numbers**: they can be singular (just one) or plural (more than one).

Nouns are found in one of six **cases**, whose main uses are as follows:

Nominative	used for the subject
Vocative	used for addressing
Accusative	used for the object
Genitive	used for 'of'
Dative	used for 'to/for'
Ablative	used for 'by/with/from'

Nouns belong to groups called **declensions**, which change their endings in the same way.

For Level 1 you need to know the first two declensions.

1.4 Nouns: 1st declension

1st declension (mainly feminine)

puella, puellae, f. = girl	Singular	Plural
Nominative	puell-a	puell-ae
Vocative	puell-a	puell-ae
Accusative	puell-am	puell-as
Genitive	puell-ae	puell-arum
Dative	puell-ae	puell-is
Ablative	puell-a	puell-is

Notice how, when a noun is listed in a vocabulary list or in a table like the one above, it is shown with its nominative singular, its genitive singular, its gender and its meaning. There is a good reason for doing things in this way, which will become apparent later.

1.5 Nouns: 2nd declension

2nd declension (mainly masculine)

dominus, domini, m. = lord/master	Singular	Plural
Nominative	domin-us	domin-i
Vocative	domin-e	domin-i
Accusative	domin-um	domin-os
Genitive	domin-i	domin-orum
Dative	domin-o	domin-is
Ablative	domin-o	domin-is

2nd declension (neuter)

bellum, belli, n. = war	Singular	Plural
Nominative	bell-um	bell-a
Vocative	bell-um	bell-a
Accusative	bell-um	bell-a
Genitive	bell-i	bell-orum
Dative	bell-o	bell-is
Ablative	bell-o	bell-is

Almost all nouns that go like **puella** are feminine. The ones you need to know for Level 1 that are masculine are:

agricola = farmer

incola = inhabitant

nauta = sailor

All nouns that you need for Level 1 that go like **dominus** are masculine.

All nouns that go like **bellum** are neuter.

1.6 Subjects and objects

The subject of a sentence is the person or thing doing the verb.
The object is the person or thing having the verb done to him/her/it.

subject	verb	object
The girl	sees	the farmer
The farmers	watch	the slaves

In Latin, the subject goes in the nominative case, the object goes in the accusative case. The verb goes at the end.

subject	object	verb
puella	agricolam	videt
agricolae	servos	spectant

In Latin, it is the ending, not the word order, that tells us whether a noun is the subject or the object.

amic**i** ludunt. = The friends play.   (N.B. amici is the subject.)

amic**os** spectant. = They watch the friends. (N.B. amicos is the object.)

? Exam-style questions

1.3   Answer the following:

(a)   Give the accusative singular of **hasta**, -ae, f. = spear.   (1)

(b)   Give the genitive plural and dative singular of **unda**, -ae, f. = wave.   (2)

(c)   **amicos**. Which case of which noun is this? Translate it.   (2)

(d)   **pericula** (acc.) means *dangers*. What change would you have to make to **pericula** if you were to write *danger* (acc.)?   (1)

(e)   **vinum** means *wine*. Explain the connection between **vinum** and the English word *vine*.   (1)

1.4   Translate into English:

(a)   incolae patriam amant.   (3)

(b)   nauta muros aedificat.   (3)

(c)   servi cibum parant.   (3)

(d)   sagittas et gladios habent.   (4)

(e)   ventum et turbas timemus.   (4)

1.5   Translate into Latin, using the vocabulary below:

(a)   The queen watches the women.   (3)

(b)   The allies attack the town.   (3)

Total marks: 30

queen = regina, -ae, f.	ally = socius, -i, m.
I watch = specto (1)	I attack = oppugno (1)
woman = femina, -ae, f.	town = oppidum, -i, n.

Sometimes a sentence seems to have no subject. Don't panic – either you haven't looked properly, or, more likely, the subject of the sentence is 'in the verb'. If a sentence has no noun in the nominative case, the subject must be a pronoun (I, you, he etc.), and will be found tucked up inside the ending of the verb. A good example of this is in question 1.4 (d) above, where the subject is 'they'.

1.7 Nouns like puer and magister

A few 2nd declension nouns end in -er and go like **puer** or **magister**:

puer, pueri, m. = boy	Singular	Plural
Nominative	puer	puer-i
Vocative	puer	puer-i
Accusative	puer-um	puer-os
Genitive	puer-i	puer-orum
Dative	puer-o	puer-is
Ablative	puer-o	puer-is

magister, magistri, m. = teacher/master	Singular	Plural
Nominative	magister	magistr-i
Vocative	magister	magistr-i
Accusative	magistr-um	magistr-os
Genitive	magistr-i	magistr-orum
Dative	magistr-o	magistr-is
Ablative	magistr-o	magistr-is

Note that magister drops its 'e' from the accusative singular onwards.

Nouns like **magister**:
ager, agri, m. = field
liber, libri, m. = book

> These nouns use exactly the same endings as **dominus** in all cases except the nominative and vocative singular.

1.8 Using all the cases

The two most important cases are the nominative and accusative, but you need to know how the others work too.

Once you have worked out which word is the subject, which is the verb, and which is the object, you will often be left with some other words, and to get these right, you need to look at what case they are in.

Vocative: addressing (talking to) someone

Remember that, when talking to someone, we put the person we are talking to in the vocative case. Nouns in the vocative will almost always be found inside inverted commas.

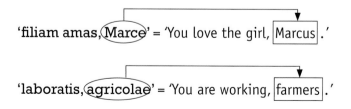

'filiam amas, Marce' = 'You love the girl, Marcus.'

'laboratis, agricolae' = 'You are working, farmers.'

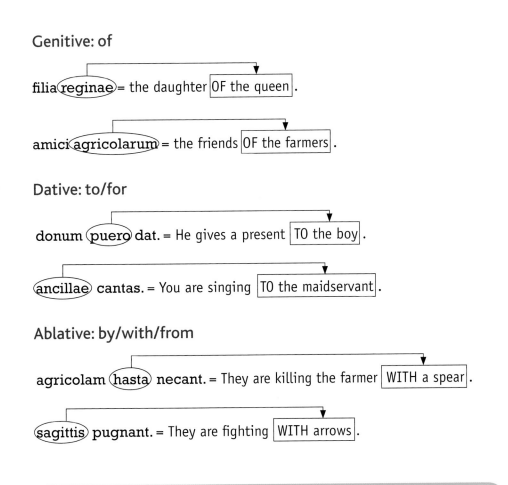

Genitive: of

filia reginae = the daughter OF the queen.

amici agricolarum = the friends OF the farmers.

Dative: to/for

donum puero dat. = He gives a present TO the boy.

ancillae cantas. = You are singing TO the maidservant.

Ablative: by/with/from

agricolam hasta necant. = They are killing the farmer WITH a spear.

sagittis pugnant. = They are fighting WITH arrows.

Many of the cases use the same endings, so it is very easy to muddle them up if you are not careful. Take particular care with the ending -ae which could be genitive singular, dative singular, nominative plural or vocative plural, depending on how the noun is being used in the sentence.

The genitive plural is easy: if the noun ends in -orum or -arum, it is genitive plural.

poetarum = of the poets

nuntiorum = of the messengers

templorum = of the temples

? Exam-style questions

1.6 Translate into English:

(a) dea vinum incolis dat. (4)

(b) servus cibum domino parat. (4)

(c) sagittas sociorum timemus. (3)

(d) librum magistro legis. (3)

(e) 'ancillas, domine, non terres!' (4)

1.7 Study the sentences in 1.6 and answer the questions below.

(a) From sentence 1.6 (a) give, in Latin, one example of each of the following:

    (i) a 1st declension noun (1)

    (ii) a 2nd declension noun (1)

(b) **domino** in sentence 1.6 (b): in which case is this noun? (1)

(c) **sagittas** in sentence 1.6 (c): in which case is this noun? (1)

(d) **legis** in sentence 1.6 (d): what part of which verb is this? (1)

(e) **terres** in sentence 1.6 (e): give the Latin object of this verb. (1)

(f) In sentence 1.6 (e) above, we are told that *you terrify the maidservants* – **ancillas terres**. What change would be needed to **terres** if you were to write *they terrify* the maidservants? (1)

(g) Using the vocabulary given below, translate into Latin:

    (i) You (sing.) fear the farmers. (2)

    (ii) The masters free the slaves. (3)

Total marks: 30

I fear = timeo (2)

farmer = agricola, -ae, m.

master = dominus, -i, m.

I free = libero (1)

slave = servus, -i, m.

★ Make sure you know

★ The present tense of amo, moneo, rego, audio and capio.

★ The declension of puella, dominus, bellum, puer and magister.

★ The use of the six cases: nominative, vocative, accusative, genitive, dative, ablative.

★ The difference between a subject and an object, and how to know which is which in a sentence.

Test yourself ✓

Before moving on to the next chapter, make sure you can answer the following. The answers are given at the back of the book.

1 Give the present infinitive of **capio** (3½).

2 In what case is the Latin subject of a sentence written?

3 In what case is the Latin object of a sentence written?

4 Give the 3rd person plural of the present tense of **venio** (4).

5 **verborum**. In which case is this word, and what does it mean?

2.1 Adjectives: bonus

Adjectives describe nouns and, in Latin, must 'agree' with the noun they describe in case, gender and number.

Many adjectives decline like **bonus**.

bonus, bona, bonum = good			
Singular	**Masculine**	**Feminine**	**Neuter**
Nominative	bon-us	bon-a	bon-um
Vocative	bon-e	bon-a	bon-um
Accusative	bon-um	bon-am	bon-um
Genitive	bon-i	bon-ae	bon-i
Dative	bon-o	bon-ae	bon-o
Ablative	bon-o	bon-a	bon-o
Plural			
Nominative	bon-i	bon-ae	bon-a
Vocative	bon-i	bon-ae	bon-a
Accusative	bon-os	bon-as	bon-a
Genitive	bon-orum	bon-arum	bon-orum
Dative	bon-is	bon-is	bon-is
Ablative	bon-is	bon-is	bon-is

The masculine of **bonus** goes like **dominus**.

The feminine goes like **puella**.

The neuter goes like **bellum**.

2.2 Agreement of adjectives

Adjectives 'agree' with the noun they describe in gender, case and number. If the noun is masculine, nominative plural, so must the adjective be.

Examples

puellarum bonarum = of the good girls

magnos gladios habemus. = We have big swords.

pueros laetos spectas. = You watch the happy boys.

2.3 Adjectives in -er

Make sure you have learnt the three adjectives which end in -er, and behave like either **puer** or **magister**, i.e. either dropping their 'e' or not.

miser, misera, miserum = wretched   keeps the 'e'
pulcher, pulchra, pulchrum = beautiful   drops the 'e'
vester, vestra, vestrum = your   drops the 'e'

> Adjectives very often, though not always, rhyme with the nouns they describe.

? **Exam-style questions**

2.1 Translate into English:

(a) dominus malus servum punit. (4)

(b) dea irata equos terret. (4)

(c) muros magnos aedificamus. (3)

(d) filiam magistri noti amo. (4)

(e) ancillas pulchras non videtis. (4)

2.2 Study the sentences above and answer the following:

(a) In sentence 2.1 (a) above, with which noun does **malus** agree? (1)

(b) In sentence 2.1 (b) above, which gender is the word **irata**? (1)

(c) In sentence 2.1 (c) above, which case is **magnos**, and why? (2)

(d) In sentence 2.1 (d) above, which word is the adjective? (1)

(e) In sentence 2.1 (e) above: **pulchras**. What is the nominative, masculine singular of this adjective? (1)

Total marks: 25

2.4 The verb sum = 'to be'

The verb 'to be' is irregular and goes as follows:

esse = to be	
sum	I am
es	You (singular) are
est	He/she/it is
sumus	We are
estis	You (plural) are
sunt	They are

2.5 sum + complement

The verb **sum** is followed by a complement: a noun or adjective in the same case, gender and number as the subject, to which it refers.

Examples

murus altus est. = The wall is high.

feminae laetae sunt. = The women are happy.

domini validi sunt. = The masters are strong.

'tuti sumus, amici.' = 'We are safe, friends.'

2.6 Prepositions

Prepositions are little words that tell us something about the position of a noun.

Some are followed by the accusative case, some by the ablative.

Prepositions + accusative

ad (+ acc.)	to/towards
in (+ acc.)	into/on to
contra (+ acc.)	against
per (+ acc.)	through
prope (+ acc.)	near
trans (+ acc.)	across

Examples

ad murum ambulamus. = We walk towards the wall.

in templum venis. = You come into the temple.

contra Romanos festinant. = They hurry against the Romans.

per undas navigant. = They sail through the waves.

prope oppidum habitat. = He lives near the town.

Prepositions + ablative

a (or ab) (+ abl.)	by/from
cum (+ abl.)	with
de (+ abl.)	down from/concerning
ex (or e) (+ abl.)	out of
in (+ abl.)	in/on

Examples

ab agris festino. = I hurry from the fields.

cum amicis ambulo. = I walk with the friends.

ex oppido festinamus. = We hurry out of the town.

agricola in aqua est. = The farmer is in the water.

in (+ acc.) = into/on to

in (+ abl.) = in/on

Examples

in aquam = into the water

in aqua = in the water

2.3 Translate into English:

    (a) in aquam currunt. (3)

    (b) ex aqua festinant. (3)

    (c) per vias ambulamus. (3)

    (d) cum amicis luditis. (3)

    (e) propter bellum perterriti sunt. (4)

2.4 Answer the following:

    (a) In sentence 2.3 (a) above, in which case is the word **aquam** and why? (2)

    (b) In sentence 2.3 (b) above, which word is the preposition? Translate it. (2)

    (c) In sentence 2.3 (c) above, **per vias** means *through the streets*. What change would be needed to these words if you wished to write *through the street*? (2)

    (d) In sentence 2.3 (d) above, in which case is **amicis**, and why? (2)

    (e) In sentence 2.3 (e) above, by which case is the preposition **propter** followed in Latin? (1)

Total marks: 25

2.7 Imperatives

To give an order, we use the imperative. These are found in the singular form if you are talking to one person, or the plural if you are talking to more than one.

Singular	ama	mone	rege	audi	cape
Plural	amate	monete	regite	audite	capite

Examples

'audi magistrum, Marce!' = 'Listen to the master, Marcus!'

'audite agricolam, servi!' = 'Listen to the farmer, slaves!'

An imperative will almost always be found inside inverted commas. And note that the word in the vocative rarely comes at the beginning of the sentence.

? Exam-style questions

2.5 Study the following passage and answer the questions below in English.

1 ubi <u>Graeci</u> ad oppidum Troiam tandem
veniunt, muros statim oppugnant et cum
<u>Troianis</u> diu pugnant. bellum <u>longum</u> est.
Graeci Troianos proeliis saevis magnopere
5 terrent et multos necant. dei tamen, quod
oppidum Troiam amant, multum auxilium
Troianis dant. Graeci igitur muros oppidi
non intrant. iam fessi sunt et ad patriam
suam navigare cupiunt.

Graeci, -orum, m. pl. =the Greeks

Troiani, -orum, m. pl. =the Trojans
longus, -a, -um = long

Common Entrance Practice Paper 2002–2003, adapted

(a) *ubi Graeci ad oppidum Troiam tandem veniunt* … (lines 1–2).

Where do the Greeks come to? (1)

(b) *… muros statim oppugnant …* (line 2)

What do they immediately do when they get there? (1)

(c) *… cum Troianis diu pugnant. bellum longum est.* (lines 2–3)

How long does the fighting go on? (1)

(d) *Graeci Troianos proeliis saevis magnopere terrent …* (lines 4–5)

How do the Greeks unsettle the Trojans? (1)

(e) *dei tamen, quod oppidum Troiam amant, multum auxilium Troianis dant.* (lines 5–7)

Why do the gods help the Trojans? (1)

2.6 Translate the passage into good English. (10)

2.7 Study the passage and answer the questions below in English.

(a) From the passage give, in Latin, one example of each of the following:

(i) an adjective (1)
(ii) a preposition followed by the accusative (1)

(b) **oppidum** (line 1): in which case is this noun? Why? (2)

(c) **Troianos** (line 4): in which case is this noun? (1)

(d) **saevis** (line 4): with which noun does this adjective agree, and in which case is it? (2)

(e) **sunt** (line 8): which part of which verb is this? Translate it. (2)

(f) In line 8, we are told that the Greeks *are tired* – **fessi sunt**. If you were to say *the Greek* (singular) *is tired*, what change would be necessary to the word **fessi**? (1)

(g) Using the vocabulary given below, translate into Latin:

(i) We hear the goddess. (2)
(ii) The boys read the books. (3)

Total marks: 30

I hear = audio (4)

goddess = dea, -ae, f.

boy = puer, -i, m.

I read = lego, -ere, legi, lectum (3)

book = liber, libri, m.

15

★ Make sure you know

★ The declension of bonus.

★ How adjectives agree with the nouns they describe.

★ The verb sum.

★ The use of prepositions.

★ How imperatives work.

Test yourself ✔

Before moving on to the next chapter, make sure you can answer the following. The answers are given at the back of the book.

1 If an adjective is used in Latin to describe a noun, what happens to the case, gender and number of the adjective?

2 What is the Latin for 'he is' and 'we are'?

3 Which case in Latin is used after the following prepositions: ad, per, prope and trans?

4 Which case in Latin is used after the following prepositions: sub, de, ex and cum?

5 Why does care need to be taken with the Latin preposition in?

3.1 Verbs: the imperfect tense

The imperfect tense refers to an action that *happened (over a period of time), was happening* or *used to happen* in the past. The endings for all five regular conjugations are essentially the same:

1st	2nd	3rd	4th	Mixed
amare = to love	monere = to warn	regere = to rule	audire = to hear	capere = to capture
ama-bam	mone-bam	reg-ebam	audi-ebam	cap-iebam
ama-bas	mone-bas	reg-ebas	audi-ebas	cap-iebas
ama-bat	mone-bat	reg-ebat	audi-ebat	cap-iebat
ama-bamus	mone-bamus	reg-ebamus	audi-ebamus	cap-iebamus
ama-batis	mone-batis	reg-ebatis	audi-ebatis	cap-iebatis
ama-bant	mone-bant	reg-ebant	audi-ebant	cap-iebant

The endings -bam, -bas, -bat, -bamus, -batis, -bant are the same for all, and are very easy to recognise. The vowel(s) before these endings change from conjugation to conjugation, but should cause you no real trouble.

Examples

vocabam = I called/was calling/used to call

clamabatis = you (plural) shouted/were shouting/used to shout

videbant = they saw/were seeing/used to see

? Exam-style questions

3.1 Translate into English:

(a) feminae miserae non dormiebant. (4)

(b) muros magnos spectabamus. (3)

(c) nuntius libros ad dominum iratum portabat. (6)

(d) socii cum Romanis saevis pugnabant. (5)

(e) cum amicis meis ludebam et cantabam. (6)

3.2 Answer the following:

(a) In sentence 3.1 (a) above, in which tense is **dormiebant**? (1)

(b) **spectabamus**, in sentence 3.1 (b) above: what is the first person singular, present tense of this verb? (1)

(c) In sentence 3.1 (c), **portabat** means (he) *was carrying*. What change would be required to the word **portabat** if we wished to say *he is carrying*? (1)

(d) In sentence 3.1 (d), **pugnabant** means (they) *were fighting*. How would you say in Latin *they are fighting*? (1)

(e) Look at sentences 3.1 (a) to (e). Write down all the verbs in the imperfect tense and, for each one, give its present infinitive. (12)

Total marks: 40

3.2 Imperfect of sum

The verb 'to be' in the imperfect tense is formed as follows:

eram	I was
eras	you (singular) were
erat	he/she/it was
eramus	we were
eratis	you (plural) were
erant	they were

The forms **erat** and **erant** are very common, and should cause you no real difficulty.

Romanus laetus erat. = The Roman was happy.

Claudia et Iulia ancillae erant. = Claudia and Julia were maidservants.

3.3 Adverbs

Adverbs are used to describe verbs, telling us *where*, *when* or *how* something is done, e.g. quickly, slowly, often etc. They do not decline or change in any way. Examples are given below:

statim	immediately
magnopere	greatly
bene	well
semper	always
diu	for a long time
numquam	never
mox	soon

Examples

dominus **semper** clamabat. = The master was **always** shouting.

servus **diu** laborabat. = The slave was working **for a long time**.

puellae cum pueris **semper** pugnant. = Girls **always** fight with boys.

3.4 Subordinate clauses

Two useful Latin words are **ubi** = when and **quod** = because. Using these two little words, we can read and write sentences that tell us *when* things were happening and *why* they were happening. The bits of the sentence which tell us *when* and *why* are called subordinate clauses, because they are subordinate to (or less important than) the main part of the sentence. Subordinate clauses are often separated from the rest of the sentence using commas.

> pueri, ubi in agro laborabant, cantabant. = The boys, when they were working in the field, were singing.
> agricola, quod laetus est, cantat. = The farmer is singing because he is happy.

Notice how the 'ubi clause' or the 'quod clause' is often tucked inside the rest of the sentence, like the jam in a sandwich.

Notice also that there are various ways of translating these types of sentences. For example, the first sentence above could be translated 'When the boys were working in the field, they were singing.'

The trick is to work out carefully what it means and then write the translation that sounds most natural.

> At Level 1, when you see the words **ubi** or **quod**, you are probably going to be told either *when* something happened or *why* it happened.

3.5 Pronouns

Make sure you know the following pronouns, found in the nominative or accusative case.

	Singular	Plural
Nominative	ego = I	nos = we
Accusative	me = me	nos = us
Nominative	tu = you	vos = you
Accusative	te = you	vos = you

> Pronouns are used in the nominative for emphasis (where we might use italics), and in the accusative where they stand as the object of the verb, or with prepositions.
>
> e.g. **ego** magnus sum sed **tu** parvus es. = *I* am big but *you* are small.
>
> **ad me** ambulabat. = He was walking towards me.

Examples

ego dominus magnus sum. = **I** am a great master.

tu servos semper vocas. = **You** are always calling the slaves.

magister **me** numquam laudat. = The teacher never praises **me**.

vos diu spectabant. = They were watching **you** for a long time.

3.3 Translate into English:

(a) agricolae, quod in agris semper laborabant, fessi erant. (6)

(b) regina, ubi nos regebat, semper laeta erat. (6)

(c) me, quod bene cantabam, saepe laudabant. (6)

(d) Romani, quod fortiter pugnabant, nos semper superabant. (6)

(e) poeta, ubi in templo cantabat, numquam iratus erat. (6)

3.4 Answer the following:

(a) In sentence 3.3 (a) above, give and translate an adverb. (2)

(b) In sentence 3.3 (b) above, what part of which verb is **erat**? (2)

(c) In sentence 3.3 (c) above, give an example of a personal pronoun, and translate it. (2)

(d) In sentence 3.3 (d) above, write down the Latin subject and object of the verb **superabant**. (2)

(e) In sentence 3.3 (e) above, with which noun does the adjective **iratus** agree? What would **iratus** become if the subject of the sentence were feminine singular? (2)

Total marks: 40

3.5 Study the following passage and answer the questions below in English.

1 post longum bellum Graeci Troianos superare cupiebant. itaque equum aedificare constituunt. equum prope oppidum ponunt et ad insulam
5 discedunt. in equo erant multi Graeci. Troiani, ubi equum vident, hastas ad eum iaciunt. nocte tamen Graeci ex equo celeriter descendunt et oppidum delent.

Graeci, -orum, m. pl. = the Greeks
Troiani, -orum, m. pl. = the Trojans

eum = it (the horse)
nocte = in the night
descendunt = they climb down

Common Entrance Practice Paper 2002–2003, adapted

(a) *post longum bellum Graeci … equum aedificare constituunt.* (lines 1–3)

What do the Greeks decide to do after the long war? (2)

(b) *equum prope oppidum ponunt et ad insulam discedunt.* (lines 3–5)

Where do they put the horse, and what do they do then? (3)

(c) *in equo erant multi Graeci.* (line 5)

Who was in the horse? (2)

(d) *Troiani, ubi equum vident, hastas ad eum iaciunt.* (lines 6–7)

What do the Trojans do when they see the horse? (2)

(e) *nocte tamen Graeci ex equo celeriter descendunt et oppidum delent.* (lines 7–8)

Explain what happens in the night. (4)

3.6 Translate the passage into good English. (10)

3.7 Study the passage and answer the questions below.

(a) From the passage give, in Latin, one example of each of the following:

(i) a verb in the imperfect tense (1)

(ii) an adverb (1)

(b) **discedunt** (line 5): in which person, number and tense is this verb? (2)

(c) **equo** (line 5): in which case is this noun, and why? (2)

(d) **erant** (line 5): which part of which verb is this? Translate it. (3)

(e) **iaciunt** (line 7): what is the subject of this verb? What is the object? (2)

(f) In lines 6–7, we are told that the Trojans *throw spears* – hastas … iaciunt. If you were to say the Greeks throw *a spear*, what change would be necessary to the word **hastas**? (1)

(g) Using the vocabulary given below, translate into Latin:

    (i) He builds a temple. (2)

    (ii) The farmers watch the horse. (3)

Total marks: 40

I build = aedifico (1)	I watch = specto (1)
temple = templum, -i, n.	horse = equus, -i, m.
farmer = agricola, -ae, m.	

★ Make sure you know

★ The imperfect tense of regular verbs.

★ The imperfect tense of sum.

★ How adverbs work.

★ The use of pronouns in the nominative and accusative cases.

Test yourself ✓

Before moving on to the next chapter, make sure you can answer the following. The answers are given at the back of the book.

1 Write out the imperfect tense of sum.

2 Give the 3rd person singular, imperfect tense of intro (1), rideo (2), bibo (3), venio (4) and iacio (3½).

3 Why might a personal pronoun be used in Latin in the nominative case?

4 Give two uses of personal pronouns in Latin in the accusative case.

5 Which of the following do NOT decline in Latin: 1st declension nouns, adjectives like **bonus**, personal pronouns, adverbs, prepositions, conjunctions?

4.1 The perfect tense

The final tense you need to learn for Level 1 is the perfect tense, which tells us what *happened* or *has happened* in the past. It refers to a completed action, unlike the imperfect tense which refers to a continuous or ongoing action.

1st	2nd	3rd	4th	Mixed
amare = to love	monere = to warn	regere = to rule	audire = to hear	capere = to capture
amav-i	monu-i	rex-i	audiv-i	cep-i
amav-isti	monu-isti	rex-isti	audiv-isti	cep-isti
amav-it	monu-it	rex-it	audiv-it	cep-it
amav-imus	monu-imus	rex-imus	audiv-imus	cep-imus
amav-istis	monu-istis	rex-istis	audiv-istis	cep-istis
amav-erunt	monu-erunt	rex-erunt	audiv-erunt	cep-erunt

The perfect tense endings are the same for all conjugations, and are added to the perfect stem. To find the perfect stem of a verb, you need to know its principal parts.

4.2 Principal parts

All verbs have principal parts, and when revising you should make sure you know them all. For Level 1, you do not need to know the 4th principal part, but it is much easier to learn them all together, rather than coming back later to add the 4th.

amo	amare	amavi	amatum	I love
moneo	monere	monui	monitum	I warn/advise
rego	regere	rexi	rectum	I rule
audio	audire	audivi	auditum	I hear
capio	capere	cepi	captum	I capture
sum	esse	fui	–	I am

The 1st principal part is the 1st person singular of the present tense: e.g. I love.

The 2nd principal part is the present infinitive: e.g. to love.

The 3rd principal part is the 1st person singular of the perfect tense: e.g. I have loved.

The 4th principal part is the supine: e.g. in order to love (N.B. **sum** has no supine).

And then at the end we have the meaning, in case you forget what the verb itself means.

The reason we are reviewing these now is that, to form the perfect tense of a verb, you have to understand the verb's principal parts. The 3rd one is sometimes a bit odd looking, but once you know it, forming the perfect tense is simple: you just chop off the -i and add the endings, -i, -isti, -it, -imus, -istis, -erunt.

> The perfect tense endings are the same for every verb, even the irregular ones like sum. But remember, you need to know the verb's perfect stem, and you can only get that right by learning the principal parts.

? **Exam-style questions**

4.1 Write out the perfect tense of the following verbs:

(a) canto, cantare, cantavi, cantatum = I sing (1)

(b) intro, intrare, intravi, intratum = I go in (1)

(c) sto, stare, steti, statum = I stand (1)

(d) iubeo, iubere, iussi, iussum = I order (1)

(e) scribo, scribere, scripsi, scriptum = I write (1)

4.2 Translate the following into English:

(a) Romani, quod irati erant, incolas puniverunt. (5)

(b) dominus cibum prope murum posuit. (5)

(c) dei et deae agricolas terruerunt. (5)

(d) nautae auxilium puero parvo dederunt. (5)

(e) amicus reginae scuta et sagittas copiis paravit. (5)

4.3 Answer the following:

(a) In sentence 4.2 (a) above, in which tense is **erant**? Give the present infinitive of this verb. (2)

(b) In sentence 4.2 (b) above, which part of which verb is **posuit**? Give its present infinitive. (3)

(c) In sentence 4.2 (c) above, **terruerunt** means *(they) terrified*. What change would be needed to **terruerunt** if you were to write *they terrify*? (1)

(d) In sentence 4.2 (d) above, find a verb in the perfect tense. What is the Latin subject of this verb? Give the verb's present infinitive. (3)

(e) In sentence 4.2 (e) above, **paravit** means *(he) prepared*. What change would be needed to **paravit** if you wished to write *they prepare*? (1)

Total marks: 40

4.3 Questions

Here are two ways of asking a question in Latin.

1 A simple (or open) question is formed by adding **-ne** to the end of the first word in the sentence.

Examples

ambulasne? = Are you walking?

puerine puellas amant? = Do the boys love the girls?

2 A specific question is formed using a questioning word, such as:
cur? = why?, **quid?** = what?, **quis?** = who? or **ubi?** = where?

Examples

quis servum necavit? = Who killed the slave?

cur in templum currebant? = Why were they running into the temple?

The word **ubi** can mean 'when' (in a subordinate clause) or 'where?' (in a question). If it is used with a question mark, it must mean 'where?'

4.4 Golden rules of Latin translation

Now would be a good time to revise the golden rules for successful translation of a simple Latin sentence. If you follow these rules, you will be safe – so follow them!

1   Look at the main verb first. It should be at the end.

2   If the verb is 1st or 2nd person, singular or plural, the subject of the verb MUST be the pronoun I, you (singular), we or you (plural).

3   If the verb is 3rd person, singular or plural, the subject of the verb will EITHER be the pronoun he/she/it or they, OR a noun in the nominative case.

4   If (and only if) the verb is 3rd person, look for a noun in the nominative case. If you find one, it must be the subject. If you don't, the subject must be he/she/it or they.

5   Translate the subject and the verb. This is the most important part of the whole sentence, and if you get this right, you should be on track to get the rest right as well.

6   Look for an object, in the accusative case. If you find one, translate it after the verb.

7   Look at the other words in the sentence, and work out which case they are in. Translate them carefully, following the case that they are in. Don't just guess, or try to cram them into the sentence in any way that might sound sensible.

There are other rules to follow, of course. For example:

8   Adjectives agree with the nouns they describe. So only put an adjective together with a noun if it is agreeing with it in gender, case and number.

9   Prepositions are followed by a noun in either the accusative or ablative case. Be sure to translate the preposition with the correct noun, which is almost always the very next word in the sentence, so this is not too tricky.

10 Some sentences have a subordinate clause tucked inside them, introduced, for example, by **ubi** or **quod**. If so, be sure to deal with these bits of the sentence carefully. Remember, the main verb will be the one at the end of the sentence, not the one tucked into the subordinate clause.

If you can keep all these rules clear in your head, particularly rules 1–5, you will not go too far wrong.

Exam-style questions

4.4 Translate into English, following the golden rules of Latin translation above.

(a) olim deus puellam pulchram punivit. (5)

(b) puerum fessum numquam monetis. (4)

(c) cum viris, quod irati erant, diu pugnabamus. (7)

(d) cum amicis ridebat ubi in templum festinaverunt. (7)

(e) cur poeta librum prope murum magnum posuit? (7)

Total marks: 30

4.5 Numbers

You need to know how to count from 1 to 10 in Latin, and to use the ordinals from 1st to 10th.

	Cardinals	Ordinals
I	unus = one	primus = first
II	duo = two	secundus = second
III	tres = three	tertius = third
IV	quattuor = four	quartus = fourth
V	quinque = five	quintus = fifth
VI	sex = six	sextus = sixth
VII	septem = seven	septimus = seventh
VIII	octo = eight	octavus = eighth
IX	novem = nine	nonus = ninth
X	decem = ten	decimus = tenth

Note that the ordinal numbers are adjectives and decline like **bonus**.

Examples

agricola cibum quintae filiae dedit. = The farmer gave food to his **fifth daughter**.

poeta secundum librum legebat. = The poet was reading his **second book**.

? **Exam-style questions**

4.5 Study the following passage and answer the questions in English.

1 olim erat puella pulchra, <u>nomine</u> Hero.   nomine = called
  multos amicos habebat et diu laeta erat.
  puerum clarum, nomine Leandrum, amabat.
  sed Leander trans undas habitabat. itaque
5 Leander puellam saepe videre non <u>poterat</u>.   poterat = (he) was able
  Leander igitur miser erat. tandem, quod
  periculum non timebat, trans undas
  <u>natare</u> constituit.   natare = to swim

Common Entrance Practice Paper June 2011, adapted

(a) *olim erat puella pulchra, nomine Hero.* (line 1)

How is Hero described? (2)

(b) *multos amicos habebat et diu laeta erat.* (line 2)

Why was she happy? (2)

(c) *multos amicos habebat et diu laeta erat.* (line 2)

Give and translate the Latin word which tells us how
long she was happy for. (2)

(d) *puerum clarum, nomine Leandrum, amabat.* (line 3)

Whom did she love, and how is he described? (2)

(e) *sed Leander trans undas habitabat.* (line 4)

Why was it not possible for Hero to see her boyfriend often? (2)

(f) *Leander igitur miser erat.* (line 6)

How did this make Leander feel? (1)

(g) *… periculum non timebat …* (line 7)

What do we learn about Leander? (2)

(h) *… trans undas natare constituit.* (lines 7–8)

How did he decide to solve the problem? (2)

4.6 Translate the following passage into good English.

1 quod venti iam boni erant, Leander <u>nocte</u>   nocte = at night
discedere statim constituit. in aquam
<u>desiluit</u> et diu trans undas ad terram puellae   desiluit = he jumped down
<u>natabat</u>. mox tamern in magnum periculum venit.   nato (1) = I swim
5 quod venti iam validi erant, undae altae saepe
Leandrum superaverunt.
tandem Leander perterritus clamavit: 'audi me,
Hero! da <u>mihi</u> auxilium!' Hero tamen in <u>ora</u>   mihi = to me
manebat et 'ubi es, Leander?' <u>frustra</u> clamabat.   ora, -ae, f. = shore
     frustra = in vain

Common Entrance Practice Paper June 2011, adapted

4.7 Study the following passage and answer the questions below.

1 tandem Hero puerum in periculo <u>inter</u>   inter (+ acc.) = among
undas vidit. perterrita erat et auxilium <u>ei</u>   ei = to him
dare constituit. undas intravit et ad puerum
<u>natavit</u>. sed undae puellam quoque   nato (1) = I swim
5 superaverunt. sic undae puerum et puellam
necaverunt.

Common Entrance Practice Paper June 2011, adapted

(a) From the passage give, in Latin, one example of each of the following:

(i) a verb in the perfect tense (1)

(ii) an adverb (1)

(b) **undas** (line 2): in which case is this noun? Why is this case used? (2)

(c) Give the genitive singular form of **undas** (line 2). (1)

(d) **constituit** (line 3): what does this word mean? Explain the connection
between **constituit** and the English word *constitution*. (3)

(e) **intravit** (line 3): in which tense is this verb? What is the first person
singular, present tense of this verb? (2)

(f) **superaverunt** (line 5): this word means *they overcame*. How would you say in Latin *they overcome* (present tense)? (1)

(g) **necaverunt** (line 6): give the Latin subject and object of this verb. (2)

(h) Using the vocabulary given below, translate into Latin:

(i) We praise the poets. (3)

(ii) The masters warn the messengers. (4)

Total marks: 65

I praise = laudo (1)   I warn = moneo (2)

poet = poeta, -ae, m.   messenger = nuntius, -i, m.

master = dominus

★ Make sure you know

★ The perfect tense of all verbs.

★ How to form questions.

★ The cardinals 1–10.

★ The ordinals 1st–10th.

Once you have thoroughly revised and mastered the background material (see Chapters 13–16), you will be ready for Latin Level 1. Good luck!

Test yourself ✔

Now that you have covered all the grammar and rules that you need for Level 1, make sure you know all the vocabulary for Level 1. Then check that you can answer the following. The answers are given at the back of the book.

1 To which conjugation do the following belong: **currebant, vocabamus, curritis, scripserunt, fecit**? Translate them.

2 To which declension do the following belong: **hastarum, muros, viam, cibus, pericula**? Translate them.

3 Give the principal parts of the following verbs: **clamo, video, mitto, venio, iacio.**

4 Write out the cardinals from one to ten in Latin.

5 Give the Latin for second, fifth, tenth.

LEVEL 2

5.1 The future tense

The future tense describes what *will happen* in the future.

1st	2nd	3rd	4th	Mixed
amare = to love	monere = to warn	regere = to rule	audire = to hear	capere = to capture
ama-bo	mone-bo	reg-am	audi-am	cap-iam
ama-bis	mone-bis	reg-es	audi-es	cap-ies
ama-bit	mone-bit	reg-et	audi-et	cap-iet
ama-bimus	mone-bimus	reg-emus	audi-emus	cap-iemus
ama-bitis	mone-bitis	reg-etis	audi-etis	cap-ietis
ama-bunt	mone-bunt	reg-ent	audi-ent	cap-ient

Notice how the first two conjugations use the endings -bo, -bis, -bit etc., while the others go -am, -es, -et.

5.2 Future of sum

The future tense of **sum** is quite easy to learn, and sort of rhymes with the -bo, -bis, -bit endings above.

ero	I shall be
eris	You (sing.) will be
erit	He/she/it will be
erimus	We shall be
eritis	You (pl.) will be
erunt	They will be

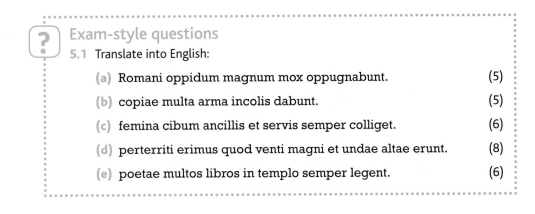

? Exam-style questions

5.1 Translate into English:

(a) Romani oppidum magnum mox oppugnabunt. (5)

(b) copiae multa arma incolis dabunt. (5)

(c) femina cibum ancillis et servis semper colliget. (6)

(d) perterriti erimus quod venti magni et undae altae erunt. (8)

(e) poetae multos libros in templo semper legent. (6)

(a) In sentence 5.1 (a), which part of which verb is **oppugnabunt**? (2)

(b) In sentence 5.1 (b), put the verb **dabunt** into the imperfect tense, keeping the person and number the same. (1)

(c) In sentence 5.1 (c), in which tense is the verb **colliget**? What would be the Latin for *they are collecting*? (2)

(d) In sentence 5.1 (d), from which verb do the forms **erimus** and **erunt** come? What would these forms become if they were in the imperfect tense? (3)

(e) In sentence 5.1 (e), which part of which verb is **legent**? (2)

Total marks: 40

5.3 3rd declension nouns: rex

A very large number of nouns of the third declension decline like **rex** if they are masculine or feminine.

rex, regis, m. = king	Singular	Plural
Nominative	rex	reg-es
Vocative	rex	reg-es
Accusative	reg-em	reg-es
Genitive	reg-is	reg-um
Dative	reg-i	reg-ibus
Ablative	reg-e	reg-ibus

Notice how the endings are added to the noun stem, which changes in the accusative singular. Make sure you know the stem of each noun. It is found by taking the **-is** off the genitive singular.

Examples

dux, ducis, m. = leader   stem = duc-

coniunx, coniugis, m./f. = husband/wife   stem = coniug-

miles, militis, m. = soldier   stem = milit-

With the stem, simply add the endings -em, -is, -i, -e etc. and you can't go wrong.

Masculine and feminine nouns like rex almost always change their 'front ends' as they move from the nominative and vocative singular forms to the accusative singular and all other forms. Getting this stem change right is crucial, so pay careful attention to it when you revise each noun.

Take great care with adjectives: when agreeing with 3rd declension nouns, these very rarely rhyme as they so often used to when we were dealing only with nouns of the 1st and 2nd declensions.

? Exam-style questions

5.3 Translate into English:

    (a) cives ducem exspectabunt. (3)

    (b) custodes copias hostium diu timebant. (5)

    (c) iuvenis laetus coniugem ducis clari laudavit. (6)

    (d) Romani senes et feminas in urbe relinquent. (5)

    (e) dux multa dona uxori pulchrae dedit. (6)

5.4 Answer the following:

    (a) In sentence 5.3 (a) above, in which case is **cives**? What is this noun's nominative singular? (2)

    (b) In sentence 5.3 (b) above, in which case is **hostium**? Give this noun's ablative plural. (2)

    (c) In sentence 5.3 (c) above, write down all the 3rd declension nouns in the sentence. (3)

    (d) In sentence 5.3 (d) above, **senes** means *old men*. Explain the connection between **senes** and the English word *senile*. (1)

    (e) In sentence 5.3 (e) above, in which case is **pulchrae** and with which noun does it agree? (2)

Total marks: 35

5.4 3rd declension nouns: nomen

rex is the most important 3rd declension noun, so make sure you know it backwards before continuing with this section. Of course not all 3rd declension nouns go like **rex**, not least because some are neuter. Many of these neuter 3rd declension nouns go like **nomen**. These essentially do what neuter nouns always do, i.e. have the same endings in the nominative, vocative and accusative, but then behave like **rex** in the genitive, dative and ablative. Notice how the stem changes in the genitive singular.

nomen, nominis, n. = name	Singular	Plural
Nominative	nomen	nomin-a
Vocative	nomen	nomin-a
Accusative	nomen	nomin-a
Genitive	nomin-is	nomin-um
Dative	nomin-i	nomin-ibus
Ablative	nomin-e	nomin-ibus

There are some variations on these two 3rd declension nouns, **rex** and **nomen**. For now, however, all you need to know is that the ablative singular of the word for sea, **mare**, is **mari**. This is a bit unexpected, but make sure you revise it so, when it crops up, you won't be caught out.

There are also nouns (such as **hostes**) that go -**ium** in the genitive plural, rather than -**um**, but again, this should not cause you any problems.

5.5 More on the golden rules of Latin translation

Now that you are dealing with 3rd declension nouns, the importance of remembering your golden rules of Latin translation (section 4.4) becomes even greater. Recognising the endings on nouns can be difficult because it assumes you know which declension the nouns belong to.

For example, consider the ending **-i** in the following sentence:

amicus pueri dona duci laeto dedit. = The friend of the boy gave gifts to the happy leader.

| **pueri** | 2nd declension | genitive singular |
| **duci** | 3rd declension | dative singular |

Or consider the ending **-is** in the following sentence:

amicus regis dona feminis dedit. = The friend of the king gave gifts to the women.

| **regis** | 3rd declension | genitive singular |
| **feminis** | 1st declension | dative plural |

Just remember, when you learn a noun, it is vital that you learn which declension it belongs to. That way, when you see it in a sentence, you will be able to work out which case it is in without resorting to guesswork.

? **Exam-style questions**

Here is a typical Level 2 passage of Latin. We will practise the three question types on the one passage of Latin (in the exam, each question will relate to a different passage).

5.5 Study the following passage and answer the questions below.

1 Orpheus erat filius dei <u>Apollinis</u>. poeta   Apollo, -inis, m. = Apollo
   bonus erat et, ubi cantabat, viri et feminae,
   etiam flumina et montes, iuvenem audire
   cupiebant. uxor Orphei, nomine Eurydice,
5 pulchra erat et diu laeta erat. olim tamen
   Eurydice cum amicis in <u>silvis</u> ambulabat.   silva, -ae, f. = wood.
   subito <u>serpens</u> feminam <u>momordit</u> et   serpens, -entis, m. = snake
   vulneravit. mox Eurydice mortua erat.   mordeo, -ere, momordi = I bite

Common Entrance Practice Paper June 2011, adapted

(a) *Orpheus erat filius dei Apollinis.* (line 1)

What are we told about Orpheus' relationship to Apollo?   (1)

(b) *... ubi cantabat, viri et feminae, etiam flumina et montes, iuvenem audire cupiebant.* (lines 2–4)

What happened when Orpheus sang?   (4)

(c) *uxor Orphei, nomine Eurydice, pulchra erat ...* (lines 4–5)

Translate the Latin adjective which describes the appearance of Orpheus' wife.   (1)

(d) *subito serpens feminam momordit et vulneravit.* (lines 7–8)

What happened when Eurydice went for a walk with her friends?   (2)

(e) *mox Eurydice mortua erat.* (line 8)

What happened to Eurydice at the end of the story?   (2)

5.6 Translate the passage into good English. (20)

5.7 Study the passage and answer the following questions.

(a) **cantabat** (line 2). In which tense is this verb? (1)

(b) Give an example from the passage of a present infinitive and translate it. (2)

(c) **flumina** (line 3). In which case is this noun, and why is this case used? (2)

(d) **erat** (line 5). Put this verb into the future tense, keeping the same person and number. (1)

(e) **amicis** (line 6). What does this word mean? Explain the connection between **amicis** and the English word *amicable*. (2)

(f) Translate the following sentences into Latin, using the vocabulary given below.

(i) The master was warning the boy. (3)
(ii) The girls hurry towards the temples. (4)

Total marks: 45

master = magister, magistri, m.	I hurry = festino (1)
I warn = moneo (2)	towards = ad (+ acc.)
boy = puer, pueri, m.	temple = templum, -i, n.
girl = puella, -ae, f.	

★ Make sure you know

★ The future tense of all verbs.

★ 3rd declension nouns like rex and nomen.

Test yourself ✔

Before moving on to the next chapter, make sure you can answer the following. The answers are given at the back of the book.

1 How does the noun **dux,** ducis, m. decline in the singular?

2 How does the noun **custos,** custodis, m. decline in the plural?

3 How does the noun **corpus,** corporis, n. decline in the singular?

4 How does the noun **vulnus,** vulneris, n. decline in the plural?

5 Write out the future tense of **moveo** (2), **cado** (3) and **facio** (3½).

6.1 The pluperfect tense

The other tense you need to know for Level 2 is the pluperfect tense, which tells us what *had happened* in the past. It is formed in the same way as the perfect tense, on the perfect stem (3rd principal part), but with a new set of endings.

1st	2nd	3rd	4th	Mixed
amare = to love	monere = to warn	regere = to rule	audire = to hear	capere = to capture
amav-eram	monu-eram	rex-eram	audiv-eram	cep-eram
amav-eras	monu-eras	rex-eras	audiv-eras	cep-eras
amav-erat	monu-erat	rex-erat	audiv-erat	cep-erat
amav-eramus	monu-eramus	rex-eramus	audiv-eramus	cep-eramus
amav-eratis	monu-eratis	rex-eratis	audiv-eratis	cep-eratis
amav-erant	monu-erant	rex-erant	audiv-erant	cep-erant

Examples

cantaverat = he had sung

acceperant = they had accepted

conspexeras = you had caught sight of

All verbs have the same endings in the pluperfect tense; and they all use the letter 'a', which is in 'had', so they are easy to recognise.

adveneram = I had arrived

collegeramus = we had collected

? Exam-style questions

6.1 Translate into English:

(a) muros statim oppugnaverant. (3)

(b) incolae hostes semper timuerant. (4)

(c) milites Romani corpora hostium trans montes portaverant. (7)

(d) nos timent quod hostes semper superamus. (6)

(e) dux diu trans terras erraverat. (5)

6.2 Answer the following:

(a) In sentence 6.1 (a), which part of which verb is **oppugnaverant**? (2)

(b) In sentence 6.1 (b), give the Latin subject and object of the verb **timuerant**. (2)

(c) In sentence 6.1 (c), in which case is **corpora**? (1)

(d) In sentence 6.1 (d), in which tense is **superamus**? How would you write *they had overcome*? (2)

(e) In sentence (e), which part of which verb is **erraverat**? Give the present infinitive of this verb. (3)

Total marks: 35

6.2 3rd declension adjectives

All the adjectives you have revised so far have gone like **bonus**, taking their endings from the 1st and 2nd declensions. Many, however, follow the 3rd declension and go like **tristis**.

tristis, triste = sad, gloomy			
Singular	Masculine	Feminine	Neuter
Nominative	trist-is	trist-is	trist-e
Vocative	trist-is	trist-is	trist-e
Accusative	trist-em	trist-em	trist-e
Genitive	trist-is	trist-is	trist-is
Dative	trist-i	trist-i	trist-i
Ablative	trist-i	trist-i	trist-i
Plural			
Nominative	trist-es	trist-es	trist-ia
Vocative	trist-es	trist-es	trist-ia
Accusative	trist-es	trist-es	trist-ia
Genitive	trist-ium	trist-ium	trist-ium
Dative	trist-ibus	trist-ibus	trist-ibus
Ablative	trist-ibus	trist-ibus	trist-ibus

Notice how the endings in the masculine and feminine are pretty much the same as **rex**, and in the neuter they are pretty much the same as **nomen**; with one huge and important difference: the ablative singular ends in -i, not -e.

Examples

agricolarum tristium = of the sad farmers

ad feminam tristem = to the sad woman

cum rege tristi = with the sad king

That ablative singular can catch you out.

Adjectives like **tristis**:

crudelis, crudele = cruel
difficilis, difficile = difficult
facilis, facile = easy
fortis, forte = strong, brave
nobilis, nobile = noble
omnis, omne = every, all

6.3 Other 3rd declension adjectives

Some 3rd declension adjectives behave in the same way as **tristis**, but start off looking rather different. These adjectives have the same ending in the nominative singular in all three genders, unlike **tristis**, which changes to **triste** in the neuter.

Examples

audax, audacis = bold

felix, felicis = happy, fortunate

ingens, ingentis = huge

sapiens, sapientis = wise

These adjectives are always written in a vocabulary list with their masculine nominative and genitive singular forms, so that you can see what the stem is.

e.g. ingens, ingentis: stem = ingent-

ingens, ingentis = huge			
Singular	Masculine	Feminine	Neuter
Nominative	ingens	ingens	ingens
Vocative	ingens	ingens	ingens
Accusative	ingent-em	ingent-em	ingens
Genitive	ingent-is	ingent-is	ingent-is
Dative	ingent-i	ingent-i	ingent-i
Ablative	ingent-i	ingent-i	ingent-i
Plural			
Nominative	ingent-es	ingent-es	ingent-ia
Vocative	ingent-es	ingent-es	ingent-ia
Accusative	ingent-es	ingent-es	ingent-ia
Genitive	ingent-ium	ingent-ium	ingent-ium
Dative	ingent-ibus	ingent-ibus	ingent-ibus
Ablative	ingent-ibus	ingent-ibus	ingent-ibus

Examples

ad templa ingentia = to the huge temples

pueros felices liberabit. = He will free the fortunate boys.

omnes cives regem sapientem amant. = All the citizens love a wise king.

? Exam-style questions

6.3 Translate into English:

(a) milites crudeles incolas fortes laudaverunt. (5)

(b) dux audax regem nobilem trans montes reduxit. (7)

(c) cibum ancillae tristi non dederat. (5)

(d) paucae feminae ducem crudelem amabant. (5)

(e) omnes agricolae templum ingens aedificare cupiverant. (6)

6.4 Answer the following:

(a) In sentence 6.3 (a) above, which adjective agrees with **incolas**? (1)

(b) In sentence 6.3 (b) above, give the Latin subject and object of the verb **reduxit**. (2)

(c) In sentence 6.3 (c), explain why **tristi** does not rhyme with **ancillae**. (1)

(d) In sentence 6.3 (d), what type of adjective is **paucae**? (1)

(e) In sentence 6.3 (e), in which case and gender is the
word **ingens**? (2)

Total marks: 35

6.4 Comparison of adjectives

Adjectives have a positive, a comparative, and a superlative.

Positive	Comparative	Superlative
long	longer	longest/very long
longus	longior	longissimus
sad	sadder	saddest/very sad
tristis	tristior	tristissimus

The superlatives are very easy to remember, because of that '-issim-' bit. These decline like **bonus**, and agree with the noun they describe in the normal way.

Examples

puellarum tristissimarum = of the very sad girls

ad vias longissimas = to the longest roads

cum milite fortissimo = with the bravest soldier

The comparatives are a bit harder, but the '-ior-' is the bit to look for. These decline like a 3rd declension adjective, with two tricky differences:

● the neuter singular goes -ius, not -e

● the ablative singular ends in -e, not -i.

In other words in the ablative singular they behave like a 3rd declension noun, not a 3rd declension adjective.

Here is a comparative adjective set out in full.

tristior, tristius = more sad			
Singular	Masculine	Feminine	Neuter
Nominative	tristior	tristior	tristius
Vocative	tristior	tristior	tristius
Accusative	tristior-em	tristior-em	tristius
Genitive	tristior-is	tristior-is	tristior-is
Dative	tristior-i	tristior-i	tristior-i
Ablative	tristior-e	tristior-e	tristior-e
Plural			
Nominative	tristior-es	tristior-es	tristior-a
Vocative	tristior-es	tristior-es	tristior-a
Accusative	tristior-es	tristior-es	tristior-a
Genitive	tristior-um	tristior-um	tristior-um
Dative	tristior-ibus	tristior-ibus	tristior-ibus
Ablative	tristior-ibus	tristior-ibus	tristior-ibus

6.5 Adjectives in -er and -lis: superlative forms

Some adjectives that end in **-er** in the positive form their superlatives in **-errimus** rather than **-issimus**.

miser	miserior	miserrimus
pulcher	pulchrior	pulcherrimus
celer	celerior	celerrimus

Some adjectives in **-lis** form their superlatives in **-illimus**.

facilis	facilior	facillimus
difficilis	difficilior	difficillimus

6.6 Irregular comparisons

Some important adjectives behave badly in the comparative and superlative and must be revised thoroughly:

Positive	Comparative	Superlative	
bonus	melior	optimus	good, better, best
malus	peior	pessimus	bad, worse, worst
magnus	maior	maximus	big, bigger, biggest
parvus	minor	minimus	small, smaller, smallest
multus	plus*	plurimus	much/many, more, most

*This word is used in the singular as a neuter noun, followed by a noun in the genitive. In the plural, it is used as an adjective and declines as follows:

	Masculine	Feminine	Neuter
Nominative	plures	plures	plura
Vocative	plures	plures	plura
Accusative	plures	plures	plura
Genitive	plurium	plurium	plurium
Dative	pluribus	pluribus	pluribus
Ablative	pluribus	pluribus	pluribus

Exam-style questions

6.5 Study the following passage and answer the questions below.

1 Achilles, <u>qui</u> fortissimus erat omnium
  Graecorum qui ante <u>Troiam</u> pugnabant,
  in <u>castris</u> iratus manebat. nam puella Briseis
  carissima duci erat, sed rex Agamemnon
5 puellam <u>abduxerat</u>. 'non iam pugnabo,'
  inquit, 'et regem crudelem puniam. nam
  Graeci <u>Troianos</u> sine me non vincent.'

qui = who
Troia, -ae, f. = Troy
castra, -orum, n. pl. = camp

abduco (3) = I steal

Troiani, -orum = Trojans

Common Entrance Practice Paper 2002–2003, adapted

(a) *Achilles … fortissimus erat omnium Graecorum …* (lines 1–2)

What are we told about Achilles? (2)

(b) *… omnium Graecorum qui ante Troiam pugnabant …* (lines 1–2)

Where were the Greeks fighting? (1)

(c) *… in castris iratus manebat.* (line 3)

What was Achilles doing in the camp? (1)

(d) *… in castris iratus manebat.* (line 3)

What mood was he in? (1)

(e) *… puella Briseis carissima duci erat, sed rex Agamemnon puellam abduxerat.* (lines 3–5)

Who was Briseis and why was Achilles upset about her? (2)

(f) *… rex Agamemnon …* (line 4)

What role did Agamemnon hold in the army? (1)

6.6 Translate the passage above into good English. (20)

6.7 Study the passage above and answer the following questions.

(a) From the passage, give one example of each of the following:

(i) a superlative adjective (1)
(ii) a verb in the future tense (1)

(b) **duci** (line 4). In which case is this word? Give the nominative singular. (2)

(c) **puniam** (line 6). Which part of which verb is this? What would it be in the 3rd person singular, perfect tense? (3)

(d) **vincent** (line 7). What does this word mean? Explain the connection between **vincent** and the English word *invincible*. (2)

(e) Using the vocabulary below, translate into Latin:

(i) The good girl loves the boys. (4)
(ii) The sailors were watching the tired farmer. (4)

Total marks: 45

good = bonus, -a, -um
girl = puella, -ae, f.
I love = amo (1)
boy = puer, -i, m.

sailor = nauta, -ae, m.
I watch = specto (1)
tired = fessus, -a, -um
farmer = agricola, -ae, m.

★ Make sure you know

★ The pluperfect tense of all verbs.

★ 3rd declension adjectives.

★ How to form and translate the comparative and superlative forms.

7.1 Pronouns

In Level 2 we have to cope with lots of pronouns, and we will start with the fact that **ego, tu, nos** and **vos** are to be found in all cases, not just the nominative and accusative. (We can ignore the vocative.) So here we go:

1st person	Singular	Plural
Nominative	ego = I	nos = we
Accusative	me = me	nos = us
Genitive	mei = of me	nostrum = of us
Dative	mihi = to me	nobis = to us
Ablative	me = with/by/from me	nobis = with/by/from us
2nd person		
Nominative	tu = you	vos = you
Accusative	te = you	vos = you
Genitive	tui = of you	vestrum = of you
Dative	tibi = to you	vobis = to you
Ablative	te = with/by/from you	vobis = with/by/from you

Examples

poeta mihi cantabat. = The poet was singing to me.

donum tibi dedi. = I gave a present to you.

With the preposition cum, a slightly odd thing happens with these pronouns. The cum is added to the end of the noun, rather than being placed before it.

me(cum) ambulat. = He is walking with me.

te(cum) ambulat. = He is walking with you.

nobis(cum) ambulat. = He is walking with us.

vobis(cum) ambulat. = He is walking with you.

7.1 Translate into English:

(a) rex mihi donum non dedit. (5)

(b) dux mecum in templo ambulabat. (4)

(c) pater meus vinum optimum tibi dabit. (6)

(d) quis scuta et sagittas nobis dabit? (5)

(e) nos auxilium vobis celeriter dedimus. (5)

7.2 Answer the following:

(a) In sentence 7.1 (a) above, in which case is **mihi**? Give its nominative singular. (2)

(b) In sentence 7.1 (b) above, give the Latin subject of the verb **ambulabat**. (1)

(c) In sentence 7.1 (c) above, what part of which word is **optimum**? Translate it. (3)

(d) In sentence 7.1 (d) above, in which case is **nobis**, and why? (2)

(e) In sentence 7.1 (e) above, in which case is **nos**, and in which case is **vobis**? (2)

Total marks: 35

7.2 The reflexive pronoun

A reflexive pronoun ends in -self and refers back to the subject.

For example, I hurt *myself*; you hurt *yourself*; he hurts *himself*.

In Latin, the 3rd person reflexive pronoun is **se** and it goes as follows, in both singular and plural:

Accusative	se	himself/herself/itself/themselves
Genitive	sui	of himself/herself/itself/themselves
Dative	sibi	to/for himself/herself/itself/themselves
Ablative	se	with/by/from himself/herself/itself/themselves

Examples

rex se necavit. = The king killed himself.

poeta sibi cantabat. = The poet was singing to himself.

servi se laudaverunt. = The slaves praised themselves.

Notice how a reflexive pronoun 'bounces back' onto the subject:

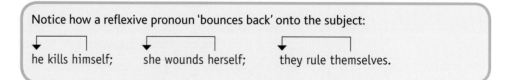

he kills himself;   she wounds herself;   they rule themselves.

7.3 More prepositions

Here are some more prepositions you need to know:

ante (+ acc.) = before propter (+ acc.) = on account of
circum (+ acc.) = around sine (+ abl.) = without
inter (+ acc.) = between sub (+ abl.) = under
post (+ acc.) = after/behind super (+ acc.) = over/on top of

7.4 Demonstrative pronouns: hic, haec, hoc

And now for even more pronouns, this time demonstrative ones, which point out the person or thing you are referring to: this one here (**hic**), that one here (**is**) and that one over there (**ille**).

hic, haec, hoc = this			
Singular	**Masculine**	**Feminine**	**Neuter**
Nominative	hic	haec	hoc
Accusative	hunc	hanc	hoc
Genitive	huius	huius	huius
Dative	huic	huic	huic
Ablative	hoc	hac	hoc
Plural			
Nominative	hi	hae	haec
Accusative	hos	has	haec
Genitive	horum	harum	horum
Dative	his	his	his
Ablative	his	his	his

Examples

hic puer malus est. = This boy is bad.

hanc puellam amamus. = We love this girl.

donum huic poetae dederunt. = They gave a present to this poet.

7.5 Demonstrative pronouns: is, ea, id

is, ea, id = that; he/she/it			
Singular	**Masculine**	**Feminine**	**Neuter**
Nominative	is	ea	id
Accusative	eum	eam	id
Genitive	eius	eius	eius
Dative	ei	ei	ei
Ablative	eo	ea	eo
Plural			
Nominative	ei	eae	ea
Accusative	eos	eas	ea
Genitive	eorum	earum	eorum
Dative	eis	eis	eis
Ablative	eis	eis	eis

is, ea, id means 'that', but it is also used to mean he/she/it, him/her/it etc.

Examples

hic rex eam ancillam spectabat. = This king was watching that maidservant.

hic rex eam spectabat. = This king was watching her.

dominus eos servos puniebat. = The master was punishing those slaves.

dominus eos puniebat. = The master was punishing them.

If is, ea, id is used in agreement with a noun, it means 'that'; if not, it means 'he/she/it'.

7.6 Demonstrative pronouns: ille, illa, illud

ille, illa, illud = that; he/she/it			
Singular	**Masculine**	**Feminine**	**Neuter**
Nominative	ille	illa	illud
Accusative	illum	illam	illud
Genitive	illius	illius	illius
Dative	illi	illi	illi
Ablative	illo	illa	illo
Plural			
Nominative	illi	illae	illa
Accusative	illos	illas	illa
Genitive	illorum	illarum	illorum
Dative	illis	illis	illis
Ablative	illis	illis	illis

NOTE: Whereas is, ea, id means 'that' as opposed to 'this', ille, illa, illud means 'that (over there)' as opposed to 'that (near me)'. It can also be used, when not agreeing with a noun, to mean he/she/it.

Examples

rex illum militem spectabat. = The king was watching that soldier.

rex illum spectabat. = The king was watching him.

? **Exam-style questions**

7.3 Translate into English:

(a) hic puer illam puellam amat. (5)

(b) rex crudelis hunc servum punivit. (5)

(c) poeta puellam amabat; ei multa dona dabat. (7)

(d) pater filium vocavit et eum salutavit. (6)

(e) dux illum gladium subito cepit et se vulneravit. (7)

7.4 Answer the following:

(a) In sentence 7.3 (a), give an example of a demonstrative pronoun. (1)

(b) In sentence 7.3 (b), in which gender is **hunc**? (1)

(c) In sentence 7.3 (c), to whom does the pronoun **ei** refer? (1)

(d) In sentence 7.3 (d), to whom does the pronoun **eum** refer? (1)

(e) In sentence 7.3 (e), what type of pronoun is **se**? (1)

Total marks: 35

7.7 Prohibitions

The imperative is used to give an order. If you wish to give a negative order, i.e. tell someone not to do something, you use **noli** (singular) or **nolite** (plural) + the infinitive.

Examples

'noli clamare, Marce!' = 'Don't shout, Marcus!'

'nolite, milites, cum civibus pugnare!' = 'Soldiers, don't fight with the citizens!'

As with imperatives, prohibitions will always be found inside inverted commas.

Exam-style questions

7.5 Study the following passage and answer the questions that follow.

1 Agamemnon, quod <u>Troiani</u>
Graecos in proelio iam superabant,
<u>sollicitus</u> erat. nuntios igitur ad
Achillem mittere constituit. nuntii ad
5 Achillem et Patroclum, comitem eius,
festinaverunt et eos ad proelium redire
iusserunt. Achilles tamen nuntiis haec
verba dixit: 'copias hostium soli
oppugnabitis. numquam
10 redibo, <u>nisi</u> rex puellam mihi tradet.
vos nunc discedere iubeo.'

Troiani, -orum, m. pl. = the Trojans

sollicitus = worried

nisi = unless

Common Entrance Practice Paper 2002–2003, adapted

(a) *Agamemnon, quod Troiani Graecos in proelio iam superabant, sollicitus erat.* (lines 1–3)

Why was Agamemnon worried? (2)

(b) *nuntios igitur ad Achillem mittere constituit.* (lines 3–4)

What did he decide to do? (2)

(c) *nuntii ad Achillem et Patroclum, comitem eius, festinaverunt …* (lines 4–6)

Who was Patroclus? (1)

(d) *nuntii ad Achillem et Patroclum, comitem eius, festinaverunt et eos ad proelium redire iusserunt.* (lines 4–7)

What did the messengers do and what were the orders they gave? (2)

(e) *Achilles tamen nuntiis haec verba dixit: 'copias hostium soli oppugnabitis. numquam redibo, nisi rex puellam mihi tradet … '* (lines 7–10)

How did Achilles respond to the messengers, and what was the condition he gave for returning to the battle? (3)

7.6 Translate the passage into good English. (20)

7.7 Study the passage and answer the following.

(a) From the passage, give three present infinitives and translate them. (6)

(b) **eius** (line 5). What case is this and from which pronoun does it come? (2)

(c) **haec** (line 7). In which case is this word? What would it be in the nominative feminine singular? (2)

(d) In lines 8–9, Achilles tells the messengers that *you will attack* the enemy alone. What change to the verb **oppugnabitis** would be necessary if he were to say to them *you have attacked*? (1)

(e) **tradet** (line 10). In which tense is this verb? Explain the connection between **tradet** and the English word *trade*. (2)

(f) Using the vocabulary below, translate into Latin:

(i) The happy boys watch the maidservants. (4)
(ii) We were reading the long book. (3)

Total marks: 50

happy = laetus, -a, -um	I read = lego (3)
boy = puer, -i, m.	long = longus, -a, -um
I watch = specto (1)	book = liber, libri, m.
maidservant = ancilla, -ae, f.	

★ Make sure you know

★ The full declension of ego, tu, nos and vos.

★ The demonstrative pronouns hic, is and ille.

★ Prohibitions using noli/nolite + infinitive.

Test yourself ✓

Before moving on to the next chapter, make sure you can answer the following. The answers are given at the back of the book.

1 Write out the masculine singular forms of hic.

2 Write out the feminine plural forms of is.

3 Write out the neuter singular forms of ille.

4 What is the Latin for *do not walk!* if you are addressing more than one person?

5 What is the Latin for *the girl will not wound herself*?

8.1 More irregular verbs: possum and eo

A few verbs in Latin are irregular, and have to be revised carefully. The verb **sum** is one; here are two more.

	possum, posse, potui = I am able	eo, ire, ii (or ivi), itum = I go
Present	possum	eo
	potes	is
	potest	it
	possumus	imus
	potestis	itis
	possunt	eunt
Future	potero	ibo
	poteris	ibis
	poterit	ibit
	poterimus	ibimus
	poteritis	ibitis
	poterunt	ibunt
Imperfect	poteram	ibam
	poteras	ibas
	poterat	ibat
	poteramus	ibamus
	poteratis	ibatis
	poterant	ibant
Perfect	potui	ii
	potuisti	isti
	potuit	iit
	potuimus	iimus
	potuistis	istis
	potuerunt	ierunt
Pluperfect	potueram	ieram
	potueras	ieras
	potuerat	ierat
	potueramus	ieramus
	potueratis	ieratis
	potuerant	ierant

In the perfect tense of **eo**, the forms **ivi, ivisti, ivit, ivimus, ivistis, iverunt** are also found, but these are more rare.

The verb **eo** is often found in compounds, which go exactly as eo, but with a prefix such as **in** or **ex**.

Examples

exeo, exire, exii, exitum = I go out

ineo, inire, inii, initum = I go in

pereo, perire, perii, peritum = I perish

transeo, transire, transii, transitum = I cross

The verb **possum** is almost always used with an infinitive, so be sure to look out for it.

e.g. Marcus scribere potest. = Marcus is able *to write*.

feminae multa templa videre poterant. = The women were able *to see* many temples.

? Exam-style questions

8.1 Translate into English:

(a) Romani hostes vincere non poterant. (4)

(b) Graeci Troianos superare sine auxilio deorum non possunt. (7)

(c) milites trans montes in patriam redierunt. (5)

(d) ancillae in templum cum domino inibunt. (4)

(e) incolae ex oppido effugere non poterant. (4)

8.2 Answer the following:

(a) In sentence 8.1 (a) above, which part of which verb is **poterant**? Put this verb into the future tense, keeping the person and number the same. (3)

(b) In sentence 8.1 (b) above, write down and translate an infinitive. (2)

(c) In sentence 8.1 (c) above, in which case is **montes**, and why? (2)

(d) In sentence 8.1 (d) above, from which verb does **inibunt** come? What is this verb's present infinitive? (2)

(e) In sentence 8.1 (e) above, give the tense of **poterant**. What change would you have to make to **poterant** if you wished to write *he will be able*? (2)

Total marks: 35

8.2 More questions: nonne and num

Sometimes when we ask a question we expect either the answer yes, or the answer no. To do this in Latin, we use **nonne** or **num**.

Expecting the answer yes: **nonne**?

Expecting the answer no: **num**?

Examples

nonne Romani hostes superabunt? = The Romans will overcome the enemy, won't they?

or

Surely the Romans will overcome the enemy?

num hostes nos superabunt? = The enemy won't overcome us, will they?

or

Surely the enemy won't overcome us?

8.3 Numbers 1–20

For Level 2 you need to know the cardinal numbers 1–20. Here they are:

I	unus = one		XI	undecim = eleven
II	duo = two		XII	duodecim = twelve
III	tres = three		XIII	tredecim = thirteen
IV	quattuor = four		XIV	quattuordecim = fourteen
V	quinque = five		XV	quindecim = fifteen
VI	sex = six		XVI	sedecim = sixteen
VII	septem = seven		XVII	septendecim = seventeen
VIII	octo = eight		XVIII	duodeviginti = eighteen
IX	novem = nine		XIX	undeviginti = nineteen
X	decem = ten		XX	viginti = twenty

The numbers from 11–17 are easy to remember; they just add **decim** (for 10) to the smaller number, sometimes squashing it in the process.

The numbers 18 and 19 mean, literally, two from twenty and one from twenty.

? Exam-style questions

8.3 Translate into English:

(a) nonne tres filios amas? (4)

(b) num bellum contra hostes geritis? (5)

(c) quattuor templa videre non poteramus. (4)

(d) quindecim milites cum duodeviginti agricolis pugnabant. (6)

(e) nonne sex montes et septem muros videre potes? (6)

Total marks: 25

8.4 Study the following passage (do not write a translation) and answer the questions below.

After defeating the Trojans, Ulysses and his comrades come to an island.

1 Ulixes comitesque Graeci, postquam Troianos
   in bello longo et saevo vicerunt, trans mare
   diu errabant. iter difficillimum erat. quod dei
   Graecos non amabant, Graeci ad <u>familias</u> statim   familia, -ae, f. = family

5 redire non poterant. olim naves Graecorum ad
insulam pulchram advenerunt. quod Graeci <u>fame</u>
iam <u>paene</u> peribant, Ulixes cibum aquamque
statim <u>quaerere</u> constituit.

fames, -is, f. = hunger
paene = almost
quaero, -ere = I search for

Common Entrance Practice Paper January 2011, adapted

(a) *Ulixes comitesque Graeci* … (line 1)

  Who travelled with Ulysses? (2)

(b) *… trans mare diu errabant.* (lines 2–3)

  What was it that the Greeks did for a long time? (2)

(c) *iter difficillimum erat.* (line 3)

  What type of journey did they have? (2)

(d) *quod dei Graecos non amabant, Graeci ad familias statim redire
non poterant.* (lines 3–5)

  Why couldn't the Greeks return to their families? (2)

(e) *olim naves Graecorum ad insulam pulchram advenerunt.* (lines 5–6)

  Where did the Greeks arrive, and how is this place described? (2)

(f) *… Ulixes cibum aquamque statim quaerere constituit.* (lines 7–8)

  What happened when they arrived there? (5)

8.5 Translate the following passage into good English.

The Greeks come across a house belonging to the goddess Circe.

1 Ulixes igitur comites in duas partes <u>divisit</u>.
plurimos nautas prope navem manere, sed
sex nautas cibum aquamque <u>quaerere</u> iussit. hi
ad villam mox advenerunt. dea pulcherrima,

divido, -ere, divisi = I
divide

quaero, -ere = I search for

5 Circe nomine, in hac <u>villa</u> habitabat. haec, ubi
Graecos vidit, eis nuntiavit: 'ego cibum
vinumque habeo. nonne intrabitis, amici?
intrate! ego vobis <u>cenam</u> optimam statim parabo!'

villa, -ae, f. = house

cena, -ae, f. = dinner

Common Entrance Practice Paper January 2011, adapted

(30)

8.6 Study the following passage and answer the questions below.

Eurylochus decides to stay outside, but the other Greeks go into Circe's house.

1 unus tamen e Graecis, Eurylochus, vir
sapientissimus, <u>villam</u> deae non intravit.
<u>extra</u> villam manere constituit. ceteri tamen
Graeci, quamquam deam timebant, quod

villa, -ae, f. = house
extra (+ acc.) = outside

5 magnopere <u>esuriebant</u>, villam eius sine
mora intraverunt.

esurio = I am hungry

Common Entrance Practice Paper January 2011, adapted

(a) From the passage give one example, in Latin, of:

  (i) a preposition followed by the ablative case (1)
  (ii) a verb in the imperfect tense (1)
  (iii) a verb in the perfect tense. (1)

(b) **vir** (line 1). What does this noun mean? Explain the connection
between **vir** and the English word *virile*. (3)

(c) **sapientissimus** (line 2). What part of speech is this? What does it
mean? (2)

(d) **deae** (line 2). In which case is this noun? Why is this case used? (2)

(e) **intraverunt** (line 6). Give the tense of this verb. Put this verb into the imperfect tense, keeping the same person and number. (2)

(f) Using the vocabulary below, translate into Latin:

(i) The farmers build a high wall. (4)
(ii) The happy girls were watching the women. (4)

Total marks: 65

farmer = agricola, -ae, m.	happy = laetus, -a, -um
I build = aedifico (1)	girl = puella, -ae, f.
high = altus, -a, -um	I watch = specto (1)
wall = murus, -i, m.	woman = femina, -ae, f.

★ Make sure you know

★ The irregular verbs possum and eo.

★ Questions introduced by nonne? or num?

★ Numbers 1–20.

Test yourself ✓

You are now ready for Level 2. Make sure that you revise all the vocabulary for Level 2 and then you are set. But before you do that, make sure you can answer the following. The answers are given at the back of the book.

1 Write out the present tense of **possum**.

2 Write out the future tense of **eo**.

3 How would you begin a question to which you expected the answer to be 'yes'?

4 How would you begin a question to which you expected the answer to be 'no'?

5 List four compounds of the verb **eo**.

LEVEL 3

9.1 The passive: present tense

When the subject of a verb is 'doing the verb', the verb is active. When the subject of a verb is 'having the verb done to him/her', it is passive. To make a verb passive in Latin, we change the endings as follows:

1st	2nd	3rd	4th	Mixed
amare = to love	monere = to warn	regere = to rule	audire = to hear	capere = to capture
am-or	mone-or	reg-or	audi-or	cap-ior
ama-ris	mone-ris	reg-eris	audi-ris	cap-eris
ama-tur	mone-tur	reg-itur	audi-tur	cap-itur
ama-mur	mone-mur	reg-imur	audi-mur	cap-imur
ama-mini	mone-mini	reg-imini	audi-mini	cap-imini
ama-ntur	mone-ntur	reg-untur	audi-untur	cap-iuntur

Examples

amamus. = We love.	**Active**
amamur. = We are loved.	**Passive**
agricolae servos spectant. = The farmers watch the slaves.	**Active**
servi ab agricolis spectantur. = The slaves are watched by the farmers.	**Passive**

These endings are really easy.

Just change the active endings to passive as follows:

Active		Passive
-o	→	-or
-s	→	-ris
-t	→	-tur
-mus	→	-mur
-tis	→	-mini
-nt	→	-ntur

9.1 Translate into English:

(a) tempestas ab omnibus nautis magnopere timetur. (5)

(b) virtus militum a principe laudatur. (4)

(c) senes et pueri parvi a custodibus crudelibus occiduntur. (5)

(d) cibus et vinum ab ancillis parantur. (4)

(e) nonne a gentibus Graeciae nos laudamur? (5)

9.2 Answer the following:

(a) In sentence 9.1 (a) above, give the Latin subject of the verb **timetur**. (1)

(b) In sentence 9.1 (b) above, in which case is **militum**, and why? (2)

(c) In sentence 9.1 (c) above, which part of which verb is **occiduntur**? Put this verb into the present active, keeping the person and number the same. (3)

(d) In sentence 9.1 (d) above, which part of which verb is **parantur**? What would this verb become if the subject were singular rather than plural? (3)

(e) In sentence 9.1 (e) above, which part of which verb is **laudamur**? Give the plural imperative (active) of this verb. (3)

Total marks: 35

9.2 The passive: future tense

The future passive endings follow the same pattern, changing -o, -s, -t to -or, -ris, -tur etc.

1st	2nd	3rd	4th	Mixed
amare = to love	monere = to warn	regere = to rule	audire = to hear	capere = to capture
ama-bor	mone-bor	reg-ar	audi-ar	cap-iar
ama-beris	mone-beris	reg-eris	audi-eris	cap-ieris
ama-bitur	mone-bitur	reg-etur	audi-etur	cap-ietur
ama-bimur	mone-bimur	reg-emur	audi-emur	cap-iemur
ama-bimini	mone-bimini	reg-emini	audi-emini	cap-iemini
ama-buntur	mone-buntur	reg-entur	audi-entur	cap-ientur

Examples

amabimus. = We shall love.		Active
amabimur. = We shall be loved.		Passive
agricolae servos spectabunt. = The farmers will watch the slaves.		Active
servi ab agricolis spectabuntur. = The slaves will be watched by the farmers.		Passive

9.3 The passive: imperfect tense

The imperfect passive endings follow the same pattern.

1st	2nd	3rd	4th	Mixed
amare = to love	monere = to warn	regere = to rule	audire = to hear	capere = to capture
ama-bar	mone-bar	reg-ebar	audi-ebar	cap-iebar
ama-baris	mone-baris	reg-ebaris	audi-ebaris	cap-iebaris
ama-batur	mone-batur	reg-ebatur	audi-ebatur	cap-iebatur
ama-bamur	mone-bamur	reg-ebamur	audi-ebamur	cap-iebamur
ama-bamini	mone-bamini	reg-ebamini	audi-ebamini	cap-iebamini
ama-bantur	mone-bantur	reg-ebantur	audi-ebantur	cap-iebantur

Examples

amabamus. = We were loving.	**Active**
amabamur. = We were being loved.	**Passive**
agricolae servos spectabant. = The farmers were watching the slaves.	**Active**
servi ab agricolis spectabantur. = The slaves were being watched by the farmers.	**Passive**

? Exam-style questions

9.3 Translate into English:

(a) praemium magnum duci optimo a rege dabatur. (6)

(b) interea custodes a principe crudeli lente puniebantur. (6)

(c) nonne labor ab ancillis geretur? (4)

(d) num animalia ex agris pellentur? (4)

(e) heri tela hostium armaque Romanorum a custodibus colligebantur. (7)

9.4 Answer the following:

(a) In sentence 9.3 (a) above, what part of which verb is **dabatur**? (2)

(b) In sentence 9.3 (b) above, in which case is **crudeli**, and why? (2)

(c) In sentence 9.3 (c) above, what is the tense of **geretur**? Put this verb into the imperfect passive, keeping the person and number the same. (2)

(d) In sentence 9.3 (d) above, what is the Latin subject of the verb **pellentur**? (1)

(e) In sentence 9.3 (e) above, put the verb **colligebantur** into the present active, keeping the person and number the same. (1)

Total marks: 35

9.4 The perfect passive

The perfect passive expresses what *has been done*, or *was done* to the subject, and involves two bits:

● the 4th principal part of the verb, the supine: changing the **-um** ending to **-us**, it becomes the perfect participle passive, or PPP.

● add to this a part of the verb **sum** and you end up with the perfect passive.

Examples

amo, amare, amavi, amatum = I love

supine: amatum

PPP: amatus

Perfect passive: amatus sum = I have been loved, I was loved

Remember, though, that the PPP is an adjective and has to agree with the subject:

	Masculine	Feminine	Neuter
Singular	amatus est	amata est	amatum est
Plural	amati sunt	amatae sunt	amata sunt

Examples

milites ad oppidum ducti sunt. = The soldiers have been led to the town.

ancillae in templum reductae sunt. = The maidservants were led back into the temple.

oppidum ab hostibus oppugnatum est. = The town has been attacked by the enemy.

To help you with all this, here is a little rhyme:

To form the perfect passive

You take the PPP

You add a part of **sum**

And make it all agree!

9.5 The pluperfect passive

This behaves in the same way as the perfect passive, except instead of adding the present tense of **sum**, we add the imperfect tense of **sum**:

amatus eram. = I (masculine) had been loved.
monita eras. = you (feminine) had been warned.
captum erat. = it (neuter) had been captured.

Exam-style questions

9.5 Study the following passage and answer the questions below.

Ulysses and his friends arrive at King Aeolus' island of Aeolia.

1 Ulixes comitesque Graeci, ubi <u>Troia</u> post decem
annos capta est, urbem deleverunt. tum ad
<u>Graeciam</u> redire et <u>familias</u> amicosque iterum
videre magnopere cupiebant. trans mare diu
5 errabant. tandem navis eorum ad insulam, Aeoliam
nomine, tempestate pulsa est. haec insula ab Aeolo,
custode ventorum, regebatur.

Troia, -ae, f. = Troy	
Graecia, -ae, f. = Greece	
familia, -ae, f. = family	

Common Entrance Practice Paper January 2011, adapted

(a) *… ubi Troia post decem annos capta est …* (lines 1–2)

How long had Ulysses spent trying to capture Troy? (1)

(b) *… urbem deleverunt.* (line 2)

What did they do when they had captured it? (1)

(c) *tum ad Graeciam redire et familias amicosque iterum videre magnopere cupiebant.* (lines 2–4)

What did the Greeks then wish to do? (3)

(d) *trans mare diu errabant.* (lines 4–5)

What did they do for a long time? (2)

(e) *tandem navis eorum ad insulam, Aeoliam nomine, tempestate pulsa est.* (lines 5–6)

Explain how the Greeks' ship ended up at Aeolia. (2)

(f) *haec insula ab Aeolo, custode ventorum, regebatur.* (lines 6–7)

Who or what was Aeolus? (1)

9.6 Translate the passage above. (20)

9.7 Study the passage above and answer the following.

(a) **comitesque** (line 1): in which case is **comites** and how is the meaning of this word affected by the addition of -**que**? (2)

(b) **capta est** (line 2): in which tense is this verb? What is its 1st person singular, present tense active? What would it be in the perfect tense active, keeping the person and number the same? (3)

(c) Give an example from the passage of the following:

(i) A verb in the imperfect passive (1)
(ii) a demonstrative pronoun (1)
(iii) a 3rd declension noun in the ablative singular (1)

(d) **pulsa est** (line 6): what part of which verb is this? Give this verb's present infinitive. Explain the connection between **pulsa est** and the English word *repulsion*. (4)

(e) Translate into Latin, using the vocabulary below.

(i) The soldiers were running into the city. (4)
(ii) All the farmers were praising the young man. (4)

Total marks: 50

soldier = miles, militis, m.	all = omnis, omne
I run = curro, -ere, cucurri	farmer = agricola, -ae, m.
into = in (+ acc.)	I praise = laudo (1)
city = urbs, urbis, f.	young man = iuvenis, -is, m.

★ Make sure you know

★ The present, future and imperfect passive of all regular verbs.

★ The perfect and pluperfect passive of all regular verbs.

★ How to form the PPP from a verb's 4th principal part.

Test yourself ✔

Before moving on to the next chapter, make sure you can answer the following. The answers are given at the back of the book.

1 What is the PPP of **facio**?

2 Give the 3rd person singular, future passive of **video**.

3 What would the verb **rexit** become if you made it passive?

4 What would the verb **victi sunt** become if you made it active?

5 Which of a verb's principal parts is used when forming the perfect passive?

10.1 5th declension nouns: res

There are five declensions in Latin, and three of them have been reviewed so far. You do not need to know the 4th declension for Level 3, so here is the 5th declension.

res, rei, f. = thing, matter, affair		
	Singular	Plural
Nominative	res	res
Vocative	res	res
Accusative	rem	res
Genitive	rei	rerum
Dative	rei	rebus
Ablative	re	rebus

Not many nouns go like this, but the other ones you need to know are:

dies, diei, m. = day
fides, fidei, f. = trust, faith
spes, spei, f. = hope

10.2 Relative pronoun: qui, quae, quod

The relative pronoun means who or which, and goes as follows:

qui, quae, quod = who/which			
Singular	Masculine	Feminine	Neuter
Nominative	qui	quae	quod
Accusative	quem	quam	quod
Genitive	cuius	cuius	cuius
Dative	cui	cui	cui
Ablative	quo	qua	quo
Plural			
Nominative	qui	quae	quae
Accusative	quos	quas	quae
Genitive	quorum	quarum	quorum
Dative	quibus	quibus	quibus
Ablative	quibus	quibus	quibus

The alternative form quis in the dative and ablative plural will not be tested at Common Entrance.

10.3 Relative clauses

A relative clause tells us something about another noun in a sentence, known as the antecedent, as follows:

puella, (quae) ad templum ambulabat, laeta erat. = The girl, (who) was walking towards the temple, was happy.

milites, (quos) rex monuerat, fortiter pugnabant. = The soldiers, (whom) the king had warned, were fighting bravely.

The relative pronoun agrees in gender and number with the antecedent. Its case is determined by the part it is playing in the relative clause. Thus, in the first example above, **quae** is the subject of **ambulabat**. In the second, **quos** is the object of **monuerat**.

> Always translate the relative clause immediately *after you have translated* the antecedent – never before.

? Exam-style questions

10.1 Translate into English:

(a) rex, qui urbem oppugnabat, a civibus timebatur. (6)

(b) regem, qui urbem oppugnabat, omnes cives timebant. (7)

(c) insula a deo, qui custos ventorum erat, regebatur. (7)

(d) omnes res urbis, quam milites defendebant, a civibus gestae sunt. (8)

(e) templum in quo poeta cantabat ab incolis aedificatum erat. (7)

10.2 Answer the following:

(a) In sentence 10.1 (a) above, which word is the antecedent? What is its gender? (2)

(b) In sentence 10.1 (b) above, in which case is **urbem**, and why is it in this case? (2)

(c) In sentence 10.1 (c) above, in which case, gender and number is **qui**? (2)

(d) In sentence 10.1 (d) above, write down and translate the relative pronoun. (2)

(e) In sentence 10.1 (e) above, in which case, gender and number is **quo**? Why is it in this case? (2)

Total marks: 45

10.4 More pronouns: ipse

ipse, ipsa, ipsum = self			
Singular	**Masculine**	**Feminine**	**Neuter**
Nominative	ipse	ipsa	ipsum
Accusative	ipsum	ipsam	ipsum
Genitive	ipsius	ipsius	ipsius
Dative	ipsi	ipsi	ipsi
Ablative	ipso	ipsa	ipso
Plural			
Nominative	ipsi	ipsae	ipsa
Accusative	ipsos	ipsas	ipsa
Genitive	ipsorum	ipsarum	ipsorum
Dative	ipsis	ipsis	ipsis
Ablative	ipsis	ipsis	ipsis

Examples

milites regem ipsum necaverunt. = The soldiers killed the king himself.

custodes reginam ipsam spectabant. = The guards were watching the queen herself.

flumina ipsa altissima erant. = The rivers themselves were very deep.

? Exam-style questions

10.3 Translate into English:

(a) spes civibus a principe ipso data est. (5)

(b) olim fidem incolarum regina ipsa laudavit. (6)

(c) milites ipsi arma hostium non timent. (6)

(d) dux ipse cibum aquamque militibus suis dedit. (7)

(e) num vos a rege ipso diu custodiebamini? (6)

10.4 Answer the following:

(a) In sentence 10.3 (a) above, with which word does **ipso** agree? (1)

(b) In sentence 10.3 (b) above, in which case, gender and number is **ipsa**, and why? (3)

(c) In sentence 10.3 (c) above, with which noun does **ipsi** agree? Translate **ipsi**. (2)

(d) In sentence 10.3 (d) above, in which case is **suis**, and why? (2)

(e) In sentence 10.3 (e) above, in which case is **vos**? Why is it in this case? (2)

Total marks: 40

10.5 More pronouns: idem

The pronoun **idem** means 'same' and goes as follows:

idem, eadem, idem = same			
Singular	Masculine	Feminine	Neuter
Nominative	idem	eadem	idem
Accusative	eundem	eandem	idem
Genitive	eiusdem	eiusdem	eiusdem
Dative	eidem	eidem	eidem
Ablative	eodem	eadem	eodem
Plural			
Nominative	eidem	eaedem	eadem
Accusative	eosdem	easdem	eadem
Genitive	eorundem	earundem	eorundem
Dative	eisdem	eisdem	eisdem
Ablative	eisdem	eisdem	eisdem

> This is essentially just is, ea, id with -dem on the end, with a few minor tweaks to the spelling.

Examples

rex ipse cibum eundem semper amabat. = The king himself always loved the same food.

magister ad oppidum cum eodem servo semper ambulabat. = The master always walked to the town with the same slave.

? Exam-style questions

10.5 Study the following passage and answer the questions below.

Aeolus gives Ulysses some help.

1 Graeci a rege Aeolo bene accepti sunt. rex ipse
   auxilium Graecis fortibus dare cupivit et statim
   <u>saccum</u>, in quem omnes venti positi erant, Ulixi   saccus, -i, m. = bag
   tradidit. tum haec verba ei dixit: 'accipe hunc
5 saccum. auxilio horum ventorum ad patriam tuam
   tutus advenire poteris.' Ulixes igitur comites suos,
   qui ad naves redire festinabant, celeriter monuit.   tempto (1) = I try
   'nolite <u>temptare</u>' inquit 'hunc saccum <u>aperire</u>.'   aperio (4) = I open

Common Entrance Practice Paper January 2011, adapted

(a) *Graeci a rege Aeolo bene accepti sunt.* (line 1)

How are the Greeks received? (1)

(b) *rex ipse auxilium Graecis fortibus dare cupivit …* (lines 1–2)

How are the Greeks described? (1)

(c) *… saccum … Ulixi tradidit.* (lines 3–4)

What did Aeolus give to Ulysses? (1)

(d) *… saccum, in quem omnes venti positi erant, Ulixi tradidit.* (lines 3–4)

What are we told about the bag that Aeolus gave to Ulysses? (2)

(e) *… comites suos, qui ad naves redire festinabant …* (lines 6–7)

What were Ulysses' companions doing? (3)

(f) ... *comites suos ... celeriter monuit. 'nolite temptare' inquit 'hunc saccum aperire'.* (lines 6–8)

What was the warning that Ulysses gave to his companions? (3)

10.6 Translate the passage on the previous page. (20)

10.7 Study the passage and answer the following:

(a) **ipse** (line 1): what case is this word, and with which noun does it agree? (2)

(b) From the passage, give one example of each of the following:

(i) a verb in the perfect passive (1)
(ii) a relative pronoun (1)
(iii) an adverb (1)

(c) **positi erant** (line 3): what is the Latin subject of this verb? Explain the connection between **positi** and the English word *position*. (2)

(d) **hunc** (line 4): give the nominative, masculine singular of this word. Translate it. (2)

(e) **monuit** (line 7): keeping the same person and number, put this verb into the imperfect tense. Translate it. (2)

(f) Translate the following sentences into Latin, using the vocabulary given below.

(i) The farmers have run into the temple. (4)
(ii) The leaders were praising the brave citizens. (4)

Total marks: 50

farmer = agricola, -ae, m.

I run = curro, -ere, cucurri

into = in (+ acc.)

temple = templum, -i, n.

leader = dux, ducis, m.

I praise = laudo (1)

brave = fortis, -e

citizen = civis, -is, m.

It is sometimes best to translate a Latin adjective as if it were an adverb.

e.g. ad patriam tutus advenit. = He arrived safely at his homeland.

★ Make sure you know

★ 5th declension nouns like res.

★ The declension of qui, quae, quod.

★ The declension of ipse and idem.

★ How to translate relative clauses.

Test yourself ✔

Before moving on to the next chapter, make sure you can answer the following. The answers are given at the back of the book.

1 What is an antecedent?

2 What is the masculine, accusative singular of **qui**?

3 What is the feminine, accusative plural of **ipse**?

4 What is the masculine, genitive plural of **idem**?

5 When translating a Latin sentence that contains a relative clause, when should you translate the relative clause?

11.1 Present participles

Present participles are adjectives formed from verbs. In English they end in -ing; in Latin they go like the 3rd declension adjective **ingens**:

amans = loving			
Singular	Masculine	Feminine	Neuter
Nominative	amans	amans	amans
Accusative	amantem	amantem	amans
Plural	Masculine	Feminine	Neuter
Nominative	amantes	amantes	amantia
Accusative	amantes	amantes	amantia

Present participles are easy to form, adding **-ns** (or **-ens** or **-iens**) to the present stem.

1st	2nd	3rd	4th	Mixed
amans = loving	monens = warning	regens = ruling	audiens = hearing	capiens =capturing

Examples

rex ancillam in templo cantantem vidit. = The king saw the maidservant singing in the temple.

agricolas in agris clamantes audivimus. = We heard the farmers (while they were) shouting in the fields.

As in the second of these two examples, it is often possible to translate a Latin present participle into English with a temporal clause.

? Exam-style questions

11.1 Translate into English:

(a) mulier senem cibum portantem vidit. (5)

(b) poeta in urbe diu habitabat, libros scribens. (6)

(c) bellum gerentes Romani a civibus semper timebantur. (6)

(d) aurum petentes multa itinera in montes fecimus. (6)

(e) regina irata ducem vinum in templo bibentem conspexit. (7)

11.2 Answer the following:

(a) In sentence 11.1 (a), what part of which verb is **portantem**? (2)

(b) In sentence 11.1 (b), in which case and gender is **scribens**? (2)

(c) In sentence 11.1 (c), from which verb does **gerentes** come? Give its present infinitive. (2)

(d) In sentence 11.1 (d), who or what is the subject of the verb **fecimus**? Give the Latin object of this verb. (2)

(e) In sentence 11.1 (e), explain the connection between **bibentem** and the English word *imbibe*. Put **bibentem** into the plural, keeping the case and gender the same. (2)

Total marks: 40

11.2 Past participle passive (PPP)

You have already met the PPP when revising the perfect passive tense. It is formed from the 4th principal part of a verb and can be used on its own as an adjective.

1st	**amatus, -a, -um** = (having been) loved
2nd	**monitus, -a, -um** = (having been) warned
3nd	**rectus, -a, -um** = (having been) ruled
4th	**auditus, -a, -um** = (having been) heard
Mixed	**captus, -a, -um** = (having been) captured

Examples

uxor regis, a militibus capta, tristissima erat. = The wife of the king, (having been) captured by the soldiers, was very sad.

filiam reginae in flumen ductam vidimus. = We saw the daughter of the queen (having been) led into the river.

Always begin by translating a PPP with the words 'having been'. Then, once you can see what it means, take them away. You may have to insert a clause, adding words such as 'after he had been', 'because he had been', or 'who had been'.

e.g. **principem captum non timuit.** = He did not fear the (having been) captured chief.

→ He did not fear the captured chief.

OR

→ He did not fear the chief who had been captured.

69

	volo, velle, volui = I wish	nolo, nolle, nolui = I do not wish
Present	volo	nolo
	vis	non vis
	vult	non vult
	volumus	nolumus
	vultis	non vultis
	volunt	nolunt
Future	volam	nolam
	voles	noles
	volet	nolet
	volemus	nolemus
	voletis	noletis
	volent	nolent
Imperfect	volebam	nolebam
	volebas	nolebas
	volebat	nolebat
	volebamus	nolebamus
	volebatis	nolebatis
	volebant	nolebant
Perfect	volui	nolui
	voluisti	noluisti
	voluit	noluit
	voluimus	noluimus
	voluistis	noluistis
	voluerunt	noluerunt
Pluperfect	volueram	nolueram
	volueras	nolueras
	voluerat	noluerat
	volueramus	nolueramus
	volueratis	nolueratis
	voluerant	noluerant

Once you are familiar with **volo**, nolo is very easy; it is just a contracted (squished) form of **non volo** and in most forms simply uses 'n' instead of 'v'.

? Exam-style questions

11.3 Translate into English:

(a) ducem in bello captum occidere nolebant. (5)

(b) agricola animalia in agrum ducta terrere noluit. (6)

(c) quis cibum ab ancillis paratum consumere vult? (6)

(d) nonne sagittas, ab incolis collectas, militibus nostris dare voletis? (8)

(e) princeps ipse novem milites ex patria pulsos iuvare volebat. (8)

11.4 Irregular verbs: fero

The verb **fero** has some very peculiar principal parts, but is actually pretty easy to deal with once you have mastered the very irregular present tense.

fero, ferre, tuli, latum = I carry	Active	Passive
Present	fero	feror
	fers	ferris
	fert	fertur
	ferimus	ferimur
	fertis	ferimini
	ferunt	feruntur
Future	feram	ferar
	feres	fereris
	feret	feretur
	etc.	etc.
Imperfect	ferebam	ferebar
	ferebas	ferebaris
	ferebat	ferebatur
	etc.	etc
Perfect	tuli	latus sum
	tulisti	latus es
	tulit	latus est
	etc.	etc.
Pluperfect	tuleram	latus eram
	tuleras	latus eras
	tulerat	latus erat
	etc.	etc.

11.5 Expressions of time

Time 'how long' is expressed by the accusative case.
Time 'when' is expressed by the ablative case.

Examples

rex patriam **multos annos** regebat. = The king ruled his country *for many years.*

Romani oppidum **tertio die** oppugnaverunt. = The Romans attacked the town *on the third day.*

11.6 Expressions of place

When going *to* or *from* named towns or small islands, no preposition is used. Instead we just use the accusative case (for motion towards) or the ablative case (for motion from).

> **Examples**
>
> milites **Romam** festinaverunt. = The soldiers hurried *to Rome.*
>
> cives **Roma** celeriter discesserunt. = The citizens departed quickly *from Rome.*

? **Exam-style questions**

11.5 Study the passage below and answer the questions that follow.

> 1 Aeneas erat clarissimus dux Troianus.
> ubi urbs eius a Graecis deleta est,
> Aeneas cum amicis Troia effugit. diu
> navigaverunt, locum tutum
> 5 petentes. tandem ad Italiam, ubi urbem
> novam aedificare volebant, advenerunt.
> multos dies ibi laetissimi habitabant.
> sed Turnus, qui rex erat Rutulorum,
> gentis saevissimae, Troianos e
> 10 patria pellere voluit.

Troianus, -a, -um = Trojan

Troia, -ae, f. = Troy

Italia, -ae, f. = Italy

Turnus, -i, m. = Turnus
Rutuli, -orum, m. pl. = the Rutulians
Troiani, -orum, m. pl. = the Trojans

Common Entrance Practice Paper June 2011, adapted

(a) *Aeneas erat clarissimus dux Troianus.* (line 1)

What are we told about Aeneas? (2)

(b) *ubi urbs eius a Graecis deleta est, Aeneas cum amicis Troia effugit.* (lines 2–3)

What caused Aeneas and his companions to flee? (2)

(c) *diu navigaverunt, locum tutum petentes.* (lines 3–5)

What were the Trojans looking for? (2)

(d) *tandem ad Italiam, ubi urbem novam aedificare volebant, advenerunt.* (lines 5–6)

What did they wish to do in Italy? (2)

(e) *multos dies ibi laetissimi habitabant.* (line 7)

How long did they live happily there? (2)

(f) *sed Turnus … Troianos e patria pellere voluit.* (lines 8–10)

What did Turnus wish to do? (2)

11.6 Translate the passage above into good English. (20)

11.7 Study the passage above and answer the following.

(a) From the passage, give one example of each of the following:

   (i) a superlative adjective (1)
   (ii) a present participle (1)
   (iii) a relative pronoun (1)

(b) **deleta est** (line 2): in which tense is this verb? Give the 1st person singular of the present indicative active of this verb. (2)

(c) **Troia** (line 3): in which case is this word and why? (2)

(d) **volebant** (line 6): what part of which verb is this? (2)

(e) **dies** (line 7): in which case is this noun, and why? (2)

(f) **pellere** (line 10): what part of the verb is this? Explain the connection between **pellere** and the English word *expel*. (2)

Total marks: 45

★ Make sure you know

- ★ Present participles.
- ★ Past participles passive (PPPs).
- ★ Irregular verbs volo, nolo and fero.
- ★ Expressions of time.
- ★ Expressions of place.

Test yourself

Before moving on to the final chapter, make sure you can answer the following. The answers are given at the back of the book.

1 How do present participles decline?

2 How do PPPs decline?

3 How is time 'how long' translated into Latin?

4 How is time 'when' translated into Latin?

5 In which situation would we *not* use a preposition when describing in Latin going to or from a place?

12.1 The imperfect subjunctive

All the tenses you have revised so far, both active and passive, have belonged to the indicative mood. These tenses have expressed what is happening, will happen, was happening, has happened etc., and deal with statements of fact. You now need to revise the subjunctive mood, which deals with what *might* happen. For Level 3, you need to know the imperfect subjunctive active, which goes as follows:

1st	2nd	3rd	4th	Mixed
amare = to love	monere = to warn	regere = to rule	audire = to hear	capere = to capture
amare-m	monere-m	regere-m	audire-m	capere-m
amare-s	monere-s	regere-s	audire-s	capere-s
amare-t	monere-t	regere-t	audire-t	capere-t
amare-mus	monere-mus	regere-mus	audire-mus	capere-mus
amare-tis	monere-tis	regere-tis	audire-tis	capere-tis
amare-nt	monere-nt	regere-nt	audire-nt	capere-nt

This is one of the easiest tenses in Latin to learn. All verbs, however irregular, go the same way. Simply add the endings -m, -s, -t, -mus, -tis, -nt to the present infinitive. It's as simple as that.

esse = to be	posse = to be able	ire = to go	velle = to wish	nolle = to not wish
esse-m	posse-m	ire-m	velle-m	nolle-m
esse-s	posse-s	ire-s	velle-s	nolle-s
esse-t	posse-t	ire-t	velle-t	nolle-t
esse-mus	posse-mus	ire-mus	velle-mus	nolle-mus
esse-tis	posse-tis	ire-tis	velle-tis	nolle-tis
esse-nt	posse-nt	ire-nt	velle-nt	nolle-nt

If you are asked about the *mood* of a verb, the three choices are indicative, imperative or subjunctive. You are not being asked about whether the verb is happy or not!

12.2 Purpose clauses

One of the most important uses of the imperfect subjunctive is to express purpose, after **ut** or **ne.** To do this we use purpose (or final) clauses.

ut + subjunctive = in order that
ne + subjunctive = in order that ... not

Examples

milites Romam contendebant **ut urbem caperent**. = The soldiers marched to Rome *in order that they might capture the city.*

cives templum intraverunt **ne hostes id delerent**. = The citizens went into the temple *in order that the enemy might not destroy it.*

? **Exam-style questions**

12.1 Translate into English:

(a) ut aquam inveniremus ad flumen statim cucurrimus. (6)

(b) ut cives terreremus urbem telis sagittisque oppugnabamus. (7)

(c) omnes agricolae, ut murum altum aedificarent, in agros festinaverunt. (7)

(d) incolae perterriti, a militibus liberati, ut se servarent Roma fugerunt. (8)

(e) agricola equum, ne eum terreret, a mari pepulit. (7)

12.2 Answer the following:

(a) In sentence 12.1 (a) above, what part of which verb is **inveniremus**? (2)

(b) In sentence 12.1 (b) above, in which case is **cives** and why? (2)

(c) In sentence 12.1 (c) above, from which verb does **aedificarent** come? Give its present infinitive. (2)

(d) In sentence 12.1 (d) above, with which noun does **liberati** agree? What is its gender? (2)

(e) In sentence 12.1 (e) above, in which mood is **terreret**, and why? (2)

Total marks: 45

12.3 Indirect command

The other main use of the imperfect subjunctive is to express an indirect command, again after **ut** or **ne**. This construction is used after the verbs **rogo, moneo, impero** (+ dative) and **persuadeo** (+ dative).

Examples

magister pueros saepe rogabat **ut libros legerent**. = The master often asked the boys *to read the books.*

dux milites monuit **ut urbem oppugnarent**. = The leader advised the soldiers to attack the city.

rex civibus imperavit **ut agros defenderent**. = The king ordered the citizens *to defend the fields.*

ego ancillae persuasi **ne cantaret**. = I persuaded the maidservant *not to sing.*

Strangely, it is not used after the verb **iubeo** (= I order) or **cogo** (= I compel), which are followed simply by a verb in the infinitive.

The verbs **impero** and **persuadeo** are followed by an indirect object in the dative case rather than by a direct object in the accusative.

e.g. dux agricolae imperavit ut fugeret. = The leader ordered the farmer to flee.

dux civibus persuasit ut fugerent. = The leader persuaded the citizens to flee.

? **Exam-style questions**

12.3 Translate into English:

(a) dominus servos saepe rogabat ut cibum pararent. (6)

(b) militibus ut flumen transirent dux Romanus imperavit. (7)

(c) heri rex verbis sapientibus nautis persuasit ut naves fortiter defenderent. (9)

(d) miles ab hostibus captus cives monuit ut ex oppido fugerent. (7)

(e) num pueris ut in flumen currerent persuasisti? (6)

12.4 Answer the following:

(a) In sentence 12.3 (a) above, in which mood is **pararent** and why? (2)

(b) In sentence 12.3 (b) above, in which case is **militibus** and why? (2)

(c) In sentence 12.3 (c) above, in which case is **sapientibus**? Why is this case used? (2)

(d) In sentence 12.3 (d) above, which part of the verb is **captus**? Give this verb's present infinitive. (2)

(e) In sentence 12.3 (e) above, what part of which verb is **persuasisti**? Explain the connection between **persuasisti** and the English word *persuasive*. (2)

Total marks: 45

12.4 Numbers 20–100 and 1000

The numbers from 20 to 100 are as follows:

20	XX	viginti
30	XXX	triginta
40	XL	quadraginta
50	L	quinquaginta
60	LX	sexaginta
70	LXX	septuaginta
80	LXXX	octoginta
90	XC	nonaginta
100	C	centum

And if you want to go higher:

| 1000 | M | mille |

12.5 A note on dum = while

The adverb **dum** = 'while' is often followed by a verb in the present tense which it is usually best to translate as if it were in the imperfect.

Example

dum in agris **laborant**, agricolae deam viderunt. = While they were working in the fields, the farmers saw the goddess.

? Exam-style questions

12.5 Study the passage below and answer the questions that follow.

On their way to Troy the Greeks abandon Philoctetes.

1 dum Graeci ad urbem Troiam navigant ut Helenam
liberarent, in itinere ad insulam advenerunt
quae <u>Lemnos</u> vocatur. ibi Philoctetem, ducem
clarissimum, a <u>serpente</u> vulneratum reliquerunt. in
5 insula novem annos solus habitans, propter vulnus
ambulare non poterat. sagittis animalia interficiebat.
nam <u>arcum</u> habebat quem ei dederat Hercules.

Lemnos = Lemnos
serpens, serpentis,
f. = snake

arcus, m. = bow (for
shooting arrows)

Common Entrance Practice Paper 2002–2003, adapted

(a) … *Graeci ad urbem Troiam navigant …* (line 1)

How did the Greeks travel to Troy? (1)

(b) … *ad urbem Troiam navigant ut Helenam liberarent …* (lines 1–2)

Why were they going there? (1)

(c) … *in itinere ad insulam advenerunt quae Lemnos vocatur.* (lines 2–3)

Where did they stop off on their way? (2)

(d) … *Philoctetem, ducem clarissimum …* (lines 3–4)

How is Philoctetes described? (2)

(e) … *Philoctetem, ducem clarissimum, a serpente vulneratum reliquerunt.* (lines 3–4)

Why did the Greeks leave Philoctetes behind? (2)

(f) *in insula novem annos solus habitans …* (lines 4–5)

For how long did he live on the island? (2)

(g) … *propter vulnus ambulare non poterat.* (lines 5–6)

From which disability did he suffer? (2)

(h) *sagittis animalia interficiebat. nam arcum habebat quem ei dederat Hercules.* (lines 6–7)

How had Hercules helped him? (3)

12.6 Translate the following passage into good English.

The prophet Calchas tells the Greeks that they will need help from Philoctetes to defeat the Trojans.

1 anno belli decimo Graeci <u>adhuc</u> fortiter pugnabant,
neque tamen muros delere aut urbem capere
poterant. tandem Calchas, <u>vates</u> Graecus
sapientissimus, '<u>Troiam</u> numquam capietis,' inquit,
5 'nisi auxilio Philoctetis.' itaque nuntios miserunt
Graeci ut Philoctetem, qui vulneratus in insula
ab amicis relictus erat, statim reducerent. eis
imperaverunt ut <u>arcum</u> quoque caperent.

adhuc = still

vates, -is, m. = prophet
Troia, -ae, f. = Troy

nisi = except

arcus, m. = bow

Common Entrance Practice Paper 2002–2003, adapted

(30)

12.7 Study the following passage and answer the questions below in English.

Philoctetes is finally persuaded to go to Troy.

1 nuntii, ubi ad insulam advenerunt, Philoctetem mox
   invenerunt. is tamen duces Graecos non amabat,
   neque Troiam navigare volebat. <u>arcus</u> tamen <u>dolo</u>   arcus, m. = a bow
   captus est nec Philoctetes ipse vivere poterat.   dolus, -i, m. = trickery
5 <u>adhuc</u> tamen redire nolebat. tandem Hercules ei   adhuc = still
   persuasit et omnes laeti Troiam navigaverunt.

Common Entrance Practice Paper 2002–2003, adapted

(a) From the passage give, in Latin, one example of each of the following:

   (i)   a verb in the perfect active   (1)
   (ii) a verb in the present infinitive   (1)
   (iii) a demonstrative pronoun   (1)

(b) **invenerunt** (line 2): what does this verb mean? Explain the connection between **invenerunt** and the English word *invention*.   (3)

(c) **duces** (line 2): put this into the singular in the same case.   (1)

(d) **amabat** (line 2): give the Latin subject and the Latin object of this verb.   (2)

(e) **dolo** (line 3): in which case is this noun? How would you translate it?   (2)

(f) In line 6 we are told that *they sailed happily to Troy* – **laeti Troiam navigaverunt**. How would the words **laeti** and **navigaverunt** change if you were to say in Latin *he* sailed happily to Troy?   (2)

(g) Using the vocabulary below, translate into Latin:

   (i)   They hurry with the companions.   (3)
   (ii) The soldiers heard the brave girl.   (4)

Total marks: 65

I hurry = festino (1)	I hear = audio, audire, audivi, auditum (4)
with = cum (+ abl.)	brave = fortis, -e
companion = comes, comitis, m.	girl = puella, -ae, f.
soldier = miles, militis, m.	

★ Make sure you know

★ The imperfect subjunctive active of regular and irregular verbs.

★ How to translate purpose clauses and indirect commands.

★ Numbers up to 100 and 1000.

Test yourself ✓

Once you have revised the non-linguistic section, you will be ready to tackle anything that a Level 3 Common Entrance paper can throw at you. Make sure you know all the words in *Latin Vocabulary for Key Stage 3 and Common Entrance*, and good luck with the exam. But just before you move on, make sure you can answer the following. The answers are given at the back of the book.

1 What construction do we use for a purpose clause?

2 What is the construction that we generally use in Latin for indirect command, and how does this differ with the verbs **iubeo** and **cogo**?

3 Write out the imperfect subjunctive of **sum**.

4 What is the Latin for one hundred?

5 What is the Latin for one thousand?

NON-LINGUISTIC
STUDIES

13 Greek mythology

This is one of the most popular sections on the exam syllabus, and the main danger is that you know too much, not too little, when you come to do the exam. There are 8 marks available for telling the story, and 2 marks for commenting on it in some way, so be sure that you are familiar with the main Greek myths and then try to cut down the facts that you wish to use in the exam so you don't run out of time. Remember, you can only get 10 marks for this section.

All of the material you need, and more, is in *Greeks and Romans* by A.M. Wright, published by Galore Park. Have fun with this – after all, it's a great break from learning all those declensions and conjugations. And below, to help you on your way, we have selected some key facts that you may wish to ensure you can trot out in an exam.

13.1 Perseus and Medusa

- King Acrisius of Argos warned by oracle that he would be killed by his grandson
- Acrisius locked his only daughter, Danae, in a tower
- Zeus fell in love with Danae and a baby, Perseus, was born
- Danae and Perseus thrown into the sea in a chest
- Washed up on the island of Seriphos
- Polydectes, king of Seriphos, ordered Perseus to fetch the head of the gorgon, Medusa
- Everyone who looked at Medusa was turned to stone
- Perseus was assisted by Hermes, who gave him a sickle, and Athene, who gave him a shiny shield
- Told where to find Medusa by the Graeae, who shared one eye and one tooth
- Perseus looked at Medusa's reflection in the shield, and cut off her head with the sickle
- Flew back to Seriphos with the head of Medusa in a bag

13.2 Jason and the Golden Fleece

- Jason was the son of Aeson, king of Iolcos
- His uncle Pelias seized the throne of Iolcos, and Jason grew up in exile in the care of Chiron, a centaur
- Jason tricked by Pelias into going in search of the Golden Fleece which belonged to Aeetes, king of Colchis
- Gathered a group of companions, including Hercules, and built a ship, the *Argo*

- Sailed through the clashing rocks and past the Harpies on the way to Colchis

- King Aeetes ordered Jason to harness two wild bulls to a plough, sow a field with a dragon's teeth and then overcome the dragon that guarded the Golden Fleece

- Medea, daughter of King Aeetes, offered to help if Jason promised to marry her

- He harnessed the bulls, protected by a magic ointment

- When Jason sowed the dragon's teeth, armed soldiers sprang up out of the soil

- Jason made them fight each other by throwing a stone into their midst

- He then put the dragon to sleep with a magic potion and took the Golden Fleece

- As Jason and Medea sailed away, Aeetes pursued them

- Medea chopped her little brother into pieces and scattered him on the waves

13.3 Theseus and the Minotaur

- Theseus was son of Aegeus, king of Athens

- Athens had been at war with Crete, whose king was Minos

- Minos kept the Minotaur, half man, half bull, in a labyrinth beneath his palace

- Every year, seven young men and seven young girls were sent from Athens to Crete to feed the Minotaur, to make amends for the death of Minos' son in war

- One year Theseus went with the other young men and girls, promising his father that he would return safely

- If he were to die, the ship would return with black sails

- In Crete he met the daughter of King Minos, Ariadne, and they fell in love

- Ariadne gave him some magic thread and a sword

- Using the sword, Theseus killed the Minotaur, and using the thread, he found his way out of the labyrinth

- Theseus and Ariadne sailed away but stopped at the island of Naxos, where Theseus deserted Ariadne

- Theseus continued on to Athens, with black sails

- Aegeus saw the black sails and threw himself into the sea

13.4 The labours of Hercules

- Hercules was the son of Zeus and Alcmene

- Hera sent Hercules mad and he killed his wife and children

- As a punishment, Hercules was ordered to complete 10 labours set by his cousin, Eurystheus, king of Mycenae

- 1st labour: to kill the Nemean lion – its hide was too tough for arrows to penetrate; he overcame it with his bare hands and used the lion's own claws to cut off the tough hide, which he wore as a cloak

- 2nd labour: to kill the Lernaean Hydra – it had many heads, and each time he cut one off, another two or three grew in its place; helped by his nephew Iolaus, who burned the stumps of the heads to prevent them growing back, he killed the Hydra and dipped his arrows in its blood, coating them in poison

- 3rd labour: to capture the Ceryneian hind – this was sacred to Artemis and could run so quickly it took him a year to catch up with it; he shot an arrow through its front feet to slow it down and then overcame the hind and took it back to Mycenae

- 4th labour: to capture the Erymanthian boar – he drove it into a snowdrift and chained it up before taking it back to Mycenae

- 5th labour: to clean the Augean stables – Augeas, king of Elis, promised to give Hercules some of his cattle if he could clean out their stables in a single day; Hercules diverted two rivers, the Alpheus and the Peneus, so that they ran through the stables and washed away all the filth

- 6th labour: the Stymphalian birds – Hercules had to drive these man-eating birds away, which he did by shaking some bronze castanets, given to him by Athene

- 7th labour: the Cretan bull – Hercules had to capture this fire-breathing bull which rampaged all over Crete

- 8th labour: to capture the horses of Diomedes – Hercules chased the horses into the sea, stunned Diomedes with his club, and fed the king to the horses; he then led the horses back to Mycenae

- 9th labour: to capture the girdle of Hippolyta, queen of the Amazons – Hippolyta willingly gave Hercules her girdle, but Hera tricked the other Amazons into thinking that Hercules was trying to kidnap Hippolyta and they attacked; Hercules killed Hippolyta and took her girdle

- 10th labour: to steal the cattle of Geryon – Hercules overcame the guards and then shot the three-headed Geryon with a single arrow before leading off the cattle

- Eurystheus was furious that Hercules had completed the 10 labours so easily, but claimed that two of them did not count: the Lernaean Hydra had been killed with the help of Iolaus, and the Augean stables had been washed by the rivers, not by him! So he set two more labours.

- 11th labour: the apples of the Hesperides – Hercules was warned that he had to kill Ladon, the dragon that guarded the apples, and that he should get Atlas (who held up the sky) to collect the apples; Hercules held the sky while Atlas collected the apples, and then Hercules tricked him into taking the sky back again

- 12th labour: the capture of Cerberus – Hercules overpowered Cerberus, the three-headed dog that guarded the Underworld, by wrapping him in his lion-skin cloak

13.5 The Trojan War

- Peleus and Thetis were getting married, and Eris, goddess of strife, was not invited to the wedding

- Eris threw a golden apple 'for the fairest' into the wedding feast

- The Judgement of Paris saw Paris, son of the king of Troy, judging between Athene, Aphrodite and Hera

- Athene offered him wisdom; Hera offered him wealth and power; Aphrodite offered him the most beautiful woman in the world – Helen, wife of Menelaus, king of Sparta

- Paris went to Sparta and carried Helen off with him back to Troy

- Menelaus gathered an army from among the Greeks to recover her, led by his brother, Agamemnon

- The Greeks beseiged Troy for ten years

- In the tenth year, Agamemnon was forced to hand back a slave girl, Chryseis, to her father, a priest of Apollo

- Agamemnon seized another slave girl, Briseis, from the Greek warrior Achilles

- Achilles refused to fight for the Greeks and, without his help, they began to lose the fighting

- Achilles' best friend Patroclus went out to fight, dressed as Achilles, but was killed

- Achilles returned to the fighting and killed Hector, the son of the Trojan king

- The Greeks then laid a trap for the Trojans: the wooden horse

- They left a wooden horse, full of soldiers, on the shore and pretended to sail away

- Laocoon, a Trojan priest, tried to warn the Trojans not to trust the Greeks, and to leave the horse where it was

- However, the Trojans brought the horse inside the city and in the night the Greek soldiers came out and set fire to the city

13.6 The wanderings of Odysseus

- After the fall of Troy, Odysseus (in Latin, Ulysses) spent 10 years sailing back to his home in Ithaca

- First he came to the land of the Lotus Eaters, where his men ate the plant and lost all desire to return home

- Then he came to the land of the Cyclopes, where he was trapped in the cave of Polyphemus

- After Polyphemus had eaten six of his men, Odysseus told him that his name was Nobody

- Odysseus blinded Polyphemus with a stake, and when the other Cyclopes came to see what was the matter, Polyphemus said that Nobody was harming him

- In the morning, Odysseus and his remaining men escaped under the bellies of Polyphemus' sheep
- Odysseus sailed away, and Polyphemus asked his father Poseidon to put a curse on him
- Odysseus came to the island of Aeolus, the king of the winds
- Aeolus gave Odysseus a bag in which every wind was trapped apart from the one he needed to blow him home to Ithaca
- Odysseus' men thought that the bag contained gold, and opened it while Odysseus was asleep – and they were promptly blown back to Aeolus
- Odysseus then came to the land of the Laestrygonians, where almost all his men were eaten and all but his own ship destroyed
- Then he came to the island where the enchantress Circe lived
- A band of men, led by Eurylochus, were turned by Circe into pigs
- Odysseus, helped by Hermes and a magic plant, moly, turned the men back into humans
- Circe advised Odysseus to visit the Underworld and consult Tiresias, the prophet
- Tiresias warned Odysseus of the dangers ahead, and told him not to harm the cattle of the Sun
- Odysseus sailed past the Sirens, having told his men to put wax in their ears and to tie him to the mast
- They then sailed past Scylla and Charybdis
- They landed on the island of the Sun god, where Odysseus warned his men not to harm the cattle
- Odysseus' men, however, ate some of the cattle, and when they sailed on, Zeus destroyed their ship with a massive storm – only Odysseus himself survived
- Odysseus was washed up on the island of Calypso where he spent seven years
- Eventually he sailed to the land of the Phaeacians where he was well received and sent on to his own home of Ithaca
- When Odysseus arrived in Ithaca, he found that his wife Penelope had been besieged by suitors, all keen to marry her
- With the help of his son Telemachus, and disguised as a beggar, he overcame the suitors and was reunited with his wife

? Exam-style questions

13.1 In the exam, you are asked to answer one of the following questions (a–b). Make sure you answer both parts (i) and (ii). For extra practice, try both questions.

(a) (i) Describe any one of Odysseus' adventures during his homecoming. (8)
(ii) Which qualities did Odysseus display during this adventure? (2)

(b) (i) Describe how Medea helped Jason to capture the Golden Fleece. (8)
(ii) What impression do you have of Medea from this episode? (2)

★ Make sure you know

★ The story of Perseus and Medusa

★ The story of Jason and the Golden Fleece

★ The story of Theseus and the Minotaur

★ The labours of Hercules

★ About the Trojan War

★ About the wanderings of Odysseus

Test yourself ✓

Before moving on to the next chapter, make sure you can answer the following. The answers are given at the back of the book.

1 Who was Danae?

2 Who was Aeetes?

3 Who was the king of Crete who fed boys and girls to his Minotaur?

4 Whose stables did Hercules have to clean as one of his labours?

5 Who was the enchantress who turned Odysseus' men into pigs?

14 The city of Rome

14.1 Romulus and Remus

- Numitor was king of Alba Longa
- Numitor's brother, Amulius, seized the throne, killed Numitor's sons and forced his only daughter, Rhea Silvia, to become a Vestal Virgin
- The god Mars fell in love with Rhea Silvia and twin boys, Romulus and Remus, were born
- Amulius had the boys thrown in the River Tiber but they survived and were found by a she-wolf
- A shepherd called Faustulus brought the twins up as his own and when they were older they drove Amulius off the throne and restored their grandfather
- They then decided to build their own city. To decide who should be king, Romulus went to the top of the Palatine Hill and Remus went to the top of the Aventine Hill. Remus saw six eagles, but Romulus saw 12
- While Romulus was building his new city, Remus jumped over the partly built walls and Romulus killed him
- The new city was called Rome, after Romulus, and was believed to have been founded in 753 BC

14.2 Horatius

- In 506 BC Tarquin the Proud, king of Rome, was driven out of the city and went for help to Lars Porsena, king of the nearby Etruscan town of Clusium
- Lars Porsena marched on Rome at the head of an army
- The Etruscans were held up at the bridge that crossed the River Tiber into the city, near the Janiculum Hill
- Here a soldier called Horatius Cocles, with two companions, stood on the bridge and prevented the Etruscans from crossing while the Romans behind him chopped down the bridge
- The two companions, Spurius Lartius and Titus Herminius, escaped back over the bridge before it fell into the river, and Horatius himself had to swim back

14.3 Mucius Scaevola

- While Lars Porsena was camped on the far side of the River Tiber from Rome, the citizens inside the city began to run short of food
- Gaius Mucius decided to kill Lars Porsena, and slipped into the Etruscan camp

- By mistake he killed the king's paymaster instead of the king
- When he was brought before the king, Gaius Mucius showed he was not afraid by thrusting his hand into the fire
- Lars Porsena was so impressed that he released Gaius Mucius, who was later known as Scaevola ('left-handed')

14.4 Cloelia

- Eventually Lars Porsena and the Romans made peace, and hostages were given to Lars Porsena
- One of these was a girl called Cloelia who with a group of fellow hostages decided to escape by swimming across the River Tiber
- Lars Porsena was furious and threatened to attack Rome if the hostages were not returned
- Cloelia returned of her own free will, and Lars Porsena was so impressed with her bravery that he allowed her to return home, taking some more of the hostages with her

14.5 Coriolanus

- Gnaeus Marcius was a Roman soldier who helped to capture the Volscian city of Corioli, and was given the name Coriolanus as a result
- Some years later, Coriolanus was expelled from Rome and he went to live with the Volsci
- Coriolanus was so angry with the Romans that he persuaded the Volsci to attack Rome
- Coriolanus had great success in battle against the Romans, and it looked as if Rome itself would soon fall to his troops
- At that stage his mother, Veturia, came to Coriolanus' camp with his wife Volumnia and two small sons, and pleaded with him not to attack the city of his fathers
- Coriolanus was shamed into withdrawing his troops, and was driven into exile by the Volsci

14.6 Manlius Torquatus

- In 361 BC Rome was being attacked by the Gauls
- During a lull in the fighting, a huge Gaul proposed that the war should be settled by a single combat between him and one of the Romans
- A brave Roman called Titus Manlius volunteered and killed the huge Gaul, taking the gold torque from around his neck, and being called Torquatus as a result
- Twenty years later, the Romans were fighting the Latins, and Manlius Torquatus' son was in the army with his father
- Manlius Torquatus was consul and in charge of the Roman army; he ordered his troops not to attack the Latins

- His son, Manlius, was provoked by the Latins and challenged one of them to single combat

- Young Manlius won the combat, but because he had disobeyed not only the consul but also his own father, Manlius Torquatus ordered that he should be killed

14.7 The theatre

- Early Roman theatres were made of wood but soon came to be built of stone

- The stage was semicircular, with a **scaena** at the back representing a two- or three-storey building

- Theatres were open air, but awnings (**velaria**) could be drawn over to keep off the sun

- The best seats were placed in the **orchestra**, nearest the stage, and were reserved for senators; entrance was free

- Actors wore masks to show the type of character they were playing; brown masks for males, white masks for females

- Old men had white hair and beards, slaves had red wigs

- Romans enjoyed comedies by Terence and Plautus

14.8 The amphitheatre

- Gladiator fights and wild beast hunts were held in the amphitheatre

- The most impressive amphitheatre was the Colosseum in Rome, holding 50,000 people

- Before gladiators fought, they saluted the emperor with the words *ave* **Caesar, morituri te salutant** ('Hail Caesar, those about to die salute you')

- Popular fights were between a **secutor**, armed with a shield and a sword, and a **retiarius**, armed with a trident and a net

- Between fights, fresh sand (**harena**) was sprinkled to soak up the blood

- Successful gladiators won their freedom and were awarded a **rudis**, a wooden sword

- Some ex-gladiators chose to become a trainer (**lanista**)

- Fights involving wild animals were popular

14.9 The circus

- Chariot racing took place in the circus, the most famous of which was the Circus Maximus in Rome

- The track ran around a central barrier called a **spina**

- At each end of the **spina** were the turning points, the **metae**

- Races normally lasted for seven laps of the track

- Most races were between teams of **quadrigae**, four-horse chariots

- The most popular teams were the **Russati** (Reds), **Veneti** (Blues), **Albati** (Whites) and **Prasini** (Greens)

- The charioteer (**auriga**) could become very rich and famous if he were successful

- The chariots started in the starting boxes (**carceres**) and the race began when the magistrate dropped his **mappa** (a cloth)

14.10 Baths

- Baths (**balneae** or **thermae**) were usually built on the same basic layout

- They were heated by an underground heating system called a hypocaust

- Bathers would begin in the **apodyterium** (changing room)

- They would then go to the **tepidarium** (warm room)

- Then they would go to the **caldarium** (hot room)

- From here, some would go to the **frigidarium** (cold room) to cool down in a cold plunge pool

- Others would prefer to go to have a massage, be covered in oil (**unguentum**) and be scraped down with a scraper called a **strigil**

- They might also exercise in the **palaestra**

- Most baths had separate areas for men and women

- Romans went to the baths to get clean but also to gossip, meet friends and conduct business

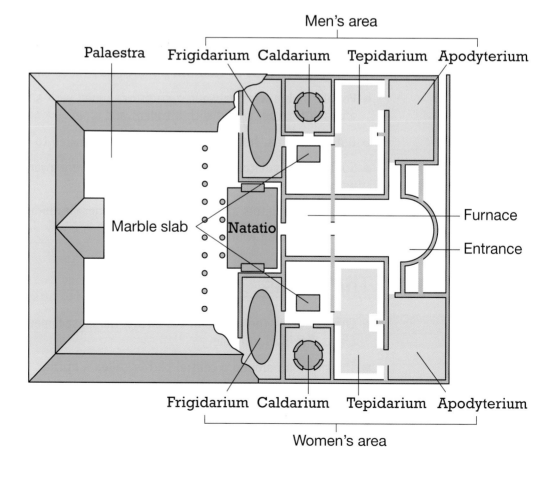

Exam-style questions

14.1 In the exam, you are only required to answer one of the following questions (a–b). Make sure you answer both parts (i) and (ii). For extra practice, try both questions.

(a) (i) What were the public baths like? Give the Latin names for some of the rooms or facilities often found in the baths. (8)

(ii) Give *two* reasons why you think Romans enjoyed going to the baths. (2)

(b) (i) Tell the story of Romulus and Remus. (8)

(ii) If you were a Roman, which part of the story would you believe and which part would you not? (2)

★ Make sure you know

- ★ The story of Romulus and Remus
- ★ How Horatius protected Rome
- ★ How Mucius Scaevola got his name
- ★ The story of Cloelia
- ★ The military achievements of Coriolanus
- ★ The story of Manlius Torquatus
- ★ What Roman theatres were like
- ★ What took place at the amphitheatre
- ★ What happened at the Roman circus
- ★ The features of Roman baths

Test yourself ✓

Before moving on to the next chapter, make sure you can answer the following. The answers are given at the back of the book.

1 Who was the mother of Romulus?

2 How did Mucius Scaevola get the name *Scaevola*?

3 What was the name of Coriolanus' mother?

4 What was the name of the structure at the back of the stage in a Roman theatre?

5 Give the Latin name for the changing room in a Roman bath.

Domestic life

15.1 Roman housing

- Poor Romans lived in blocks of flats called **insulae**

- A Roman town house was called a **domus**

- A **domus** was built around a courtyard and was entered through a **ianua** which led into the **atrium**

- In the roof of the **atrium** was a hole, or **compluvium**, which allowed rain to fall down into a pool in the middle of the floor, the **impluvium**

- In the **atrium** stood the **lararium**, which housed the household gods of the family

- Around the **atrium** were **cubicula** (bedrooms), the **tablinum** (study) and **triclinium** (dining room); there would also be a **culina** (kitchen)

- From the **atrium** one passed through into the **peristylium** (courtyard garden) where there might be two garden rooms, the **oecus** (outdoor dining room) and the **exedra** (outdoor sitting room)

- Houses were often decorated with mosaic floors, wall paintings called frescoes, and statues, often of family members

- Running water was rare, and ususally came from a fountain out in the street; there would however be a **latrina** (lavatory)

- Lighting came from oil lamps and heating came from a brazier or, in a rich man's house, a hypocaust system similar to that found in baths

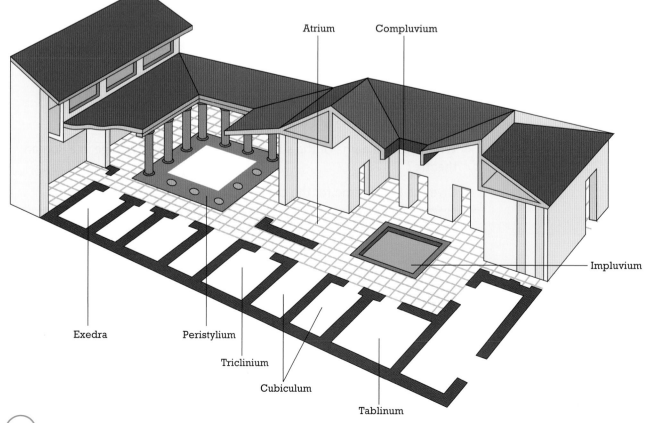

15.2 Roman food and meals

- Breakfast was called **ientaculum** and consisted of water or wine, bread, fruit, olives and honey

- Lunch was called **prandium** and would normally be a cold snack of bread, fruit, cheese, olives and dried figs

- The main meal was **cena**, which would be served in the **triclinium**, with the diners reclining on couches (**lecti**), with three couches around a circular table, and three diners per couch

- A typical **cena** might consist of three courses: **gustatio** (starter), **primae mensae** (main course) and **secundae mensae** (dessert)

- The food was a typical Mediterranean diet with lots of fish, olives and vegetables; special delicacies included stuffed dormice (**glires**), oysters, lampreys, boar and peacock

15.3 Roman clothing

- Men wore a tunic with a belt at the waist; senators wore a white tunic with a broad purple stripe down the middle, the **tunica laticlavia**; knights wore a tunic with two thin purple stripes; everyone else wore plain tunics

- Roman citizens wore a toga over their tunic: senators and priests wore a toga with a broad purple stripe, the **toga praetexta**; ordinary citizens wore a plain toga, the **toga virilis**

- If it was cold, men might wear a woollen cloak called a **lacerna** or **pallium**

- Women wore a tunic and a **stola** (dress), with a **palla** (cloak)

- Both men and women wore sandals, **soleae**

- Children wore the same as the adults, but in addition they wore a **bulla** around their neck until they came of age; boys under 16 would wear the **toga praetexta**

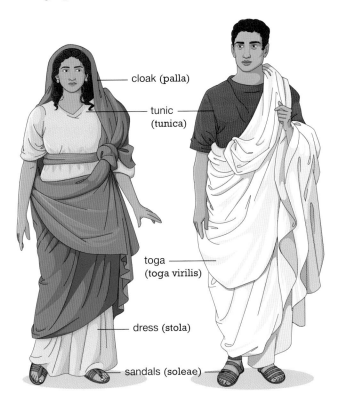

cloak (palla)

tunic (tunica)

toga (toga virilis)

dress (stola)

sandals (soleae)

15.4 Roman slavery

- Slaves could be bought from slave dealers (**venalicii**) and could be used to perform domestic duties such as cooking or cleaning, or to assist with running a business

- They would be displayed on a platform with a scroll (**titulus**), around their neck, listing their qualities

- Some slaves were owned by the state (**servi publici**) and helped with administration or maintaining public buildings

- Some slaves were forced to work in the mines or on farms

- Slaves were regarded as possessions and were sometimes very badly treated

- They could be granted their freedom (**manumissio**), often in their owners' wills, in which case they became freedmen

15.5 Life and death

- A Roman boy came of age at around the age of 14; he dedicated his **bulla** and his **toga praetexta** to the household gods, and took on the **toga virilis**; he was able to marry from the age of 14

- A Roman girl could marry from the age of 12; at her wedding (**nuptiae**) she wore a white dress (**tunica recta**), a bright orange veil (**flammeum**) and a yellow cloak (**palla**)

- After the ceremony there was a feast, the **cena nuptialis**; after this, the bride pretended not to wish to leave her parents, and the groom snatched her from her mother and took her to his home

- When a Roman died, a small coin was put in the dead person's mouth to pay Charon, the ferryman, to transport him or her to the Underworld

- Funerals could be very elaborate, with processions escorting the body to the forum where a speech (**laudatio**) in praise of the dead person might be made

- Bodies were often cremated and the ashes placed in an urn and put in the family tomb

> **?** Exam-style questions
>
> 15.1 In the exam, you are only required to answer one of the following questions (a–b). Make sure you answer both parts (i) and (ii). For extra practice, try both questions.
>
> (a) (i) How were Roman dining rooms arranged and how were meals served? (8)
>
> (ii) State *two* ways in which you might have found eating a Roman meal unfamiliar or awkward. (2)
>
> (b) (i) Describe a slave market. How were slaves advertised? (8)
>
> (ii) If you were a rich Roman, name two qualities you might look for in a new slave who would work in your house. Explain your reasons. (2)

★ Make sure you know

- ★ The different types of Roman housing
- ★ What the Romans ate
- ★ What Roman men, women and children wore
- ★ Some facts about slavery
- ★ Marriage, death and burial customs

Test yourself ✔

Before moving on to the next chapter, make sure you can answer the following. The answers are given at the back of the book.

1 Give the Latin names for the following rooms: kitchen, dining room, bedroom, lavatory

2 What type of tunic did a senator wear?

3 What was the main meal of the day for a Roman?

4 What was a freedman?

5 Who was Charon?

16 The army and Roman Britain

16.1 Army organisation

- A legion, led by a **legatus**, was made up of ten cohorts and totalled around 5300 men
- A cohort was made up of six centuries
- A century, led by a **centurio**, was made up of ten **contubernia**
- A **contubernium** was made up of eight men

16.2 Army equipment

- Soldiers carried a **gladius** (sword), a **pilum** (spear), a **pugio** (dagger) and a **scutum** (shield)
- They wore a **galea** (helmet), **lorica** (breastplate) and **caligae** (sandals)
- They carried food for three days, and tools to build a camp
- They fired a range of catapults such as the **tormentum**, **onager** and **ballista**

16.3 Army camps

- Camps (**castra**) were built on a rectangular plan, surrounded on all four sides by a **fossa** (ditch) and an **agger** (rampart)
- In the middle was the **principia**, the headquarters of the general and his staff
- The general would address the men in the camp from a tribunal or platform
- Some camps had baths (**thermae**)
- Camps were guarded by **custodes** who took turns during the four night watches (**vigiliae**), each lasting for three hours

16.4 Army tombstones

- Roman tombstones recorded information about the dead person using commonly used abbreviations
- Inscriptions usually began with DM = **dis manibus** (to the gods of the Underworld)
- Then the **praenomen, nomen** and **cognomen** were recorded
- Then the soldier's rank, legion and length of service

- Then his age
- Finally the letters HSE = **hic situs est** (here is buried)

The tombstone for Titus Calidius Severus, son of Publius

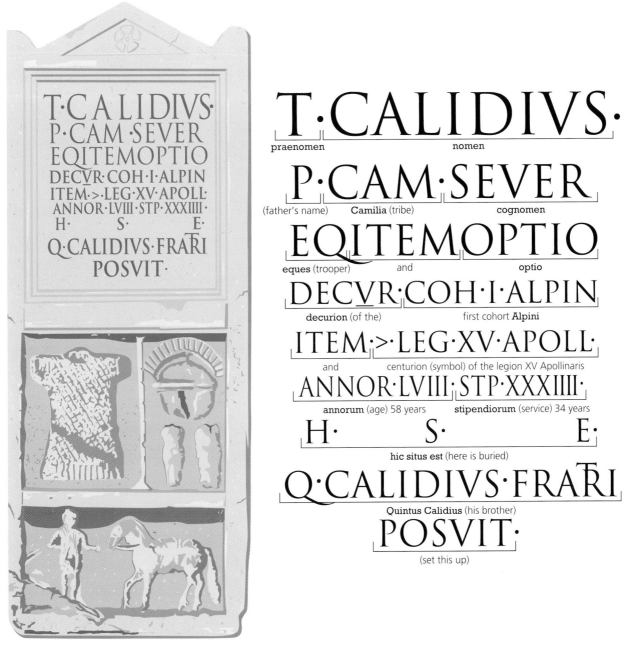

T·CALIDIVS·
praenomen   nomen

P·CAM·SEVER
(father's name)   Camilia (tribe)   cognomen

EQITEMOPTIO
eques (trooper)   and   optio

DECVR·COH·I·ALPIN
decurion (of the)   first cohort **Alpini**

ITEM·>·LEG·XV·APOLL·
and   centurion (symbol) of the legion XV Apollinaris

ANNOR·LVIII·STP·XXXIIII·
annorum (age) 58 years   stipendiorum (service) 34 years

H·   S·   E·
hic situs est (here is buried)

Q·CALIDIVS·FRATRI
Quintus Calidius (his brother)

POSVIT·
(set this up)

■ The inscription records his life and military service, with translations shown below words or groups of words

16.5 Julius Caesar in Britain

- Invaded in 55 BC but achieved very little
- Returned in 54 BC with five legions
- Crossed the Thames and defeated Cassivellaunus
- Left after a few months to put down a revolt in Gaul

- Emperor Claudius invaded in 43 AD with four legions led by Aulus Plautius

- Defeated Caratacus, king of the **Catuvellauni**, and drove him back to **Camulodunum** (Colchester)

- Romans conquered Britain from **Isca Dumnoniorum** (Exeter) in the south to **Lindum** (Lincoln) in the north

- Caratacus was captured by the Romans and sent back to Rome in chains; the Emperor Claudius was impressed by his bravery and spared his life

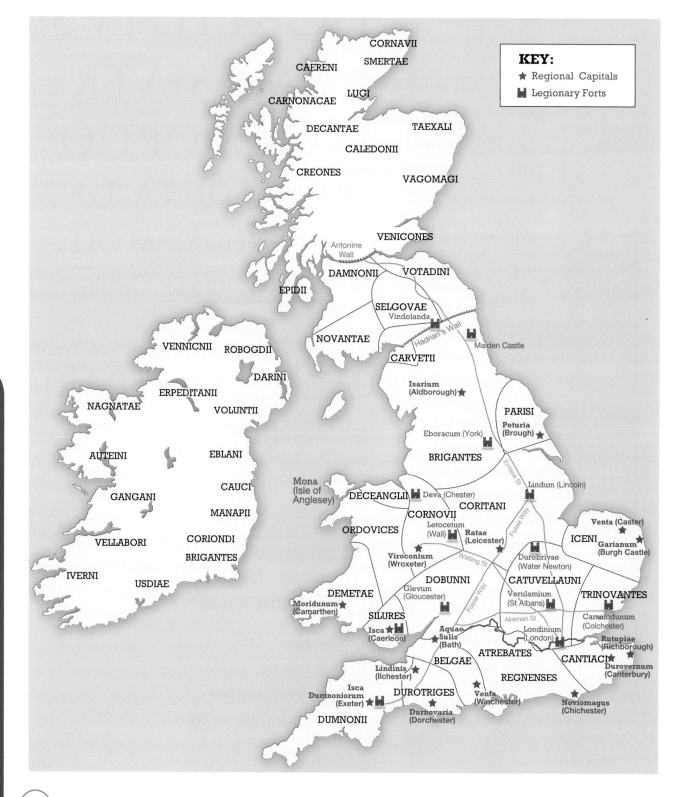

- Ten years later, Romans seized the lands of Boudicca, daughter of the king of the Iceni
- Boudicca raised a revolt against the Romans in 60 AD, burning **Camulodunum** and massacring the Roman garrison there
- Boudicca then burnt **Londinium** (London) and **Verulamium** (St Albans)
- Boudicca was eventually defeated by Roman general Suetonius Paulinus, and committed suicide

16.7 Roman towns and villas

- Roman towns grew up on the site of British settlements, or near army camps
- Some towns were **coloniae**, settlements to house retired legionaries and their families
- Towns were laid out on similar lines to army camps; in the middle was the **forum** and the **basilica**
- Towns often had temples, a theatre, baths and an amphitheatre, as well as shops and houses
- Outside towns, rich Romans and Britons loyal to Rome would live in villas (large country houses) such as the ones at Fishbourne, Bignor and Chedworth

16.8 Hadrian's Wall

- Built by the Emperor Hadrian around 122 AD to protect Britain from the fierce tribes to the north
- 117 kilometres long, stretching from the Solway Firth near Carlisle to the Tyne estuary at Newcastle
- Every mile there was a small fort or milecastle, and between every two milecastles were two watch towers
- In 126 AD 16 forts were added along the length of the wall, each housing one cohort of soldiers
- One of these forts, at Vindolanda, has been excavated; Roman tablets were found in the mud, revealing many aspects of life in a Roman camp

---

? **Exam-style questions**

16.1 In the exam, you are only required to answer one of the following questions (a–b). Make sure you answer both parts (i) and (ii). For extra practice, try both questions.

(a) (i) Tell the story of Claudius and Caratacus and how Claudius spared Caratacus. (8)

(ii) Suggest what might eventually have happened to Caratacus and his family. (2)

(b) (i) What was the plan of a Roman army camp and how was it fortified?
Name some of the buildings to be found in a large camp. (8)

(ii) Give *two* reasons why the layout of a camp was always the same in whichever country the camp was. (2)

★ Make sure you know about

- ★ The organisation of the Roman army
- ★ Equipment, camps and tombstones
- ★ Julius Caesar's invasion of Britain
- ★ Claudius' invasion of Britain
- ★ Caratacus and Boudicca
- ★ Towns and villas in Roman Britain
- ★ Hadrian's Wall

Test yourself ✓

As you finish this final chapter, make sure you can answer the following. The answers are given at the back of the book.

1 How many soldiers were there in a typical legion?

2 When did Julius Caesar first invade Britain?

3 When did Claudius invade Britain?

4 What was the name of the tribe ruled by Boudicca?

5 How long was Hadrian's Wall?

Exam-style question answers

Chapter 1

1.1 (a) Present. **festino**. (2)

   (b) **consumunt**. (1)

   (c) Present infinitive active of **scribo**. To write. (2)

   (d) Dormitory, a room in which people sleep, comes from the Latin **dormio** = I sleep. (1)

   (e) 1st person plural, present tense of **habito**. (1)

1.2 (a) **cupit**. (1)

   (b) **invenimus**. (1)

   (c) **mittis**. (1)

   (d) **rident**. (1)

   (e) **nuntiatis**. (1)

Total marks: 12

1.3 (a) **hastam**. (1)

   (b) **undarum; undae**. (2)

   (c) Accusative plural of **amicus**. (The) friends. (2)

   (d) **periculum**. (1)

   (e) Grapes, used for making wine, grow on vines. The Latin for wine is **vinum**, from which we get the word vine. (1)

1.4 (a) The inhabitants love the fatherland. (3)

   (b) The sailor builds walls. (3)

   (c) The slaves prepare the food. (3)

   (d) They have arrows and swords. (4)

   (e) We fear the wind and crowds. (4)

1.5 (a) **regina feminas spectat**. (3)

   (b) **socii oppidum oppugnant**. (3)

Total marks: 30

1.6 (a) The goddess gives wine to the inhabitants. (4)

   (b) The slave prepares food for the master. (4)

   (c) We fear the arrows of the allies. (3)

   (d) You read the book to the master. (3)

   (e) 'O master, you are not terrifying the maidservants!' (4)

1.7 (a) (i) dea or incolis. (1)

(ii) vinum. (1)

(b) Dative singular. (1)

(c) Accusative plural. (1)

(d) 2nd person singular, present tense of **lego.** (1)

(e) ancillas. (1)

(f) terrent. (1)

(g) (i) agricolas times. (2)

(ii) domini servos liberant. (3)

Total marks: 30

Chapter 2

2.1 (a) The bad master punishes the slave. (4)

(b) The angry goddess terrifies the horses. (4)

(c) We build big walls. (3)

(d) I love the daughter of the well-known master. (4)

(e) You do not see the beautiful maidservants. (4)

2.2 (a) dominus. (1)

(b) Feminine. (1)

(c) Accusative plural, because it agrees with **muros,** the object of **aedificamus.** (2)

(d) noti. (1)

(e) pulcher. (1)

Total marks: 25

2.3 (a) They run into the water. (3)

(b) They hurry out of the water. (3)

(c) We walk through the streets. (3)

(d) You play with the friends. (3)

(e) They are terrified on account of the war. (4)

2.4 (a) Accusative singular; because it follows **in** (+ acc.). (2)

(b) **ex.** Out of. (2)

(c) **per viam.** (2)

(d) Ablative plural, because it follows **cum** (+ abl.). (2)

(e) Accusative. (1)

Total marks: 25

2.5 (a) The town of Troy. (1)

(b) They attack the walls. (1)

(c) For a long time. (1)

(d) They greatly terrify them with fierce battles. (1)

(e) Because they love Troy. (1)

2.6 When the Greeks come at last to the town of Troy, they immediately attack the walls and for a long time they fight with the Trojans. The war is long. The Greeks greatly terrify the Trojans with savage battles and they kill many. The gods, however, because they love the town of Troy, give much help to the Trojans. The Greeks therefore do not enter the walls of the town. Now they are tired and want to sail to their own country. (10)

2.7 (a) (i) Any of: **longum, saevis, multos, multum, fessi, suam.** (1)

(ii) Either of: **ad oppidum; ad patriam suam.** (1)

(b) Accusative singular; because it follows **ad** (+ acc.). (2)

(c) Accusative plural. (1)

(d) **proeliis**; ablative plural. (2)

(e) 3rd person plural, present tense of **sum**. They are. (2)

(f) **fessus.** (1)

(g) (i) **deam audimus.** (2)

(ii) **pueri libros legunt.** (3)

Total marks: 30

Chapter 3

3.1 (a) The wretched women were not sleeping. (4)

(b) We were watching the big walls. (3)

(c) The messenger was carrying books to the angry master. (6)

(d) The allies were fighting with the savage Romans. (5)

(e) I was playing with my friends and singing. (6)

3.2 (a) Imperfect. (1)

(b) **specto.** (1)

(c) **portat.** (1)

(d) **pugnant.** (1)

(e) **dormiebant – dormire.**

spectabamus – spectare.

portabat – portare.

pugnabant – pugnare.

ludebam – ludere.

cantabam – cantare. (12)

Total marks: 40

3.3 (a) The farmers, because they were always working in the fields, were tired. (6)

(b) The queen was always happy when she was ruling us. (6)

(c) They often praised me because I sang well. (6)

(d) Because they fought bravely, the Romans always overcame us. (6)

(e) When he was singing in the temple, the poet was never angry. (6)

3.4 (a) semper = always. (2)

    (b) 3rd person singular, imperfect tense of **sum**. (2)

    (c) **me** = me. (2)

    (d) Subject: Romani. Object: nos. (2)

    (e) poeta. irata. (2)

Total marks: 40

3.5 (a) They decide to build a horse. (2)

    (b) They put it near the town and go away to an island. (3)

    (c) Many Greeks. (2)

    (d) They throw spears at it. (2)

    (e) The Greeks quickly climb down from the horse and destroy the town. (4)

3.6 After a long war, the Greeks wanted to overcome the Trojans. They therefore decide to build a horse. They place the horse near the town and go away to an island. In the horse there were many Greeks. The Trojans, when they see the horse, throw spears at it. In the night however the Greeks climb down quickly from the horse and destroy the town. (10)

3.7 (a) (i) **cupiebant** or **erant**. (1)

       (ii) **celeriter**. (1)

    (b) 3rd person plural, present tense. (2)

    (c) Ablative singular, because it follows **in** (+ abl.). (2)

    (d) 3rd person plural, imperfect tense of **sum**. There were. (3)

    (e) Subject: **Troiani**. Object: **hastas**. (2)

    (f) **hastam**. (1)

    (g) (i) **templum aedificat**. (2)

       (ii) **agricolae equum spectant**. (3)

Total marks: 40

Chapter 4

4.1 (a) cantavi, cantavisti, cantavit, cantavimus, cantavistis, cantaverunt. (1)

    (b) intravi, intravisti, intravit, intravimus, intravistis, intraverunt. (1)

    (c) steti, stetisti, stetit, stetimus, stetistis, steterunt. (1)

    (d) iussi, iussisti, iussit, iussimus, iussistis, iusserunt. (1)

    (e) scripsi, scripsisti, scripsit, scripsimus, scripsistis, scripserunt. (1)

4.2 (a) The Romans punished the inhabitants because they were angry. (5)

    (b) The master placed food near the wall. (5)

    (c) The gods and goddesses frightened the farmers. (5)

    (d) The sailors gave help to the small boy. (5)

    (e) The friend of the queen prepared shields and arrows for the forces. (5)

4.3 (a) Imperfect. **esse.**   (2)

(b) 3rd person singular, perfect tense of **pono. ponere.**   (3)

(c) **terrent.**   (1)

(d) **dederunt. nautae. dare.**   (3)

(e) **parant.**   (1)

Total marks: 40

4.4 (a) Once the god punished the beautiful girl.   (5)

(b) You never warn the tired boy.   (4)

(c) We were fighting for a long time with the men because they were angry.   (7)

(d) He was laughing with his friends when they hurried into the temple.   (7)

(e) Why did the poet put the book near the big wall?   (7)

Total marks: 30

4.5 (a) As a beautiful girl.   (2)

(b) Because she had many friends.   (2)

(c) **diu.** For a long time.   (2)

(d) Leander, a famous boy.   (2)

(e) Because he lived in a land across the waves.   (2)

(f) Sad.   (1)

(g) He did not fear danger.   (2)

(h) He decided to swim across the waves.   (2)

4.6 Because the winds were now good, Leander immediately decided to depart at night. He jumped down into the water and for a long time he swam across the waves towards the land of the girl. Soon however he came into great danger. Because the winds were now strong, the high waves often overcame Leander. At last, terrified, Leander cried: 'Hero, hear me! Help me!' Hero however remained on the shore and shouted in vain, 'Where are you, Leander?'   (30)

4.7 (a) (i) Any of: **vidit, constituit, intravit, natavit, superaverunt, necaverunt.**   (1)

(ii) Any of: **tandem, quoque, sic.**   (1)

(b) Accusative plural. It follows **inter** (+ acc.).   (2)

(c) **undae.**   (1)

(d) She decided. A constitution, from the Latin **constituo** = I decide, is a set of rules and regulations that have been decided upon.   (3)

(e) Perfect. **intro.**   (2)

(f) **superant.**   (1)

(g) Subject: **undae.** Object: **puerum et puellam.**   (2)

(h) (i) **poetas laudamus.**   (3)

(ii) **domini nuntios monent.**   (4)

Total marks: 65

Chapter 5

5.1 **(a)** The Romans will soon attack the large town. (5)

(b) The forces will give many weapons to the inhabitants. (5)

(c) The woman will always collect food for the maidservants and slaves. (6)

(d) We shall be terrified because the winds will be big and the waves will be high. (8)

(e) The poets will always read many books in the temple. (6)

5.2 **(a)** 3rd person plural, future tense of **oppugno**. (2)

(b) **dabant**. (1)

(c) Future. **colligunt**. (2)

(d) **sum. eramus, erant**. (3)

(e) 3rd person plural, future tense of **lego**. (2)

Total marks: 40

5.3 **(a)** The citizens will wait for the leader. (3)

(b) The guards feared the forces of the enemy for a long time. (5)

(c) The happy young man praised the wife of the famous leader. (6)

(d) The Romans will leave the the old men and the women in the city. (5)

(e) The leader gave many gifts to his beautiful wife. (6)

5.4 **(a)** Nominative plural. **civis**. (2)

(b) Genitive plural. **hostibus**. (2)

(c) **iuvenis, coniugem, ducis**. (3)

(d) As people become old, they sometimes become senile, from the Latin **senex** = old man. (1)

(e) Dative singular. **uxori**. (2)

Total marks: 35

5.5 **(a)** He was his son. (1)

(b) Men, women, rivers and mountains wanted to hear the young man sing. (4)

(c) **pulchra** = beautiful. (1)

(d) A serpent bit and wounded her. (2)

(e) She died. (2)

5.6 Orpheus was the son of the god Apollo. He was a good poet and, when he sang, men and women, even rivers and mountains, wanted to listen to the young man. Orpheus' wife, called Eurydice, was beautiful and for a long time she was happy. Once however Eurydice was walking with her friends in the woods. Suddenly a snake bit and wounded the woman. Soon Eurydice was dead. (20)

5.7 **(a)** Imperfect. (1)

(b) **audire** = to hear. (2)

(c) Nominative plural. It is the subject (along with **viri, feminae** and **montes**) of **cupiebant**. (2)

(d) erit. (1)

(e) Friends. Amicable, from the Latin **amicus** = friend, means friendly. (2)

(f) **(i)** magister puerum monebat. (3)

    (ii) puellae ad templa festinant. (4)

Total marks: 45

Chapter 6

6.1 **(a)** They had immediately attacked the walls. (3)

(b) The inhabitants had always feared the enemy. (4)

(c) The Roman soldiers had carried the bodies of the enemy across the mountains. (7)

(d) They fear us because we always overcome the enemy. (6)

(e) The leader had wandered for a long time across the lands. (5)

6.2 **(a)** 3rd person plural, pluperfect tense of **oppugno**. (2)

(b) Subject: **incolae**. Object: **hostes**. (2)

(c) Accusative plural. (1)

(d) Present. **superaverant**. (2)

(e) 3rd person singular, pluperfect tense of **erro**. **errare**. (3)

Total marks: 35

6.3 **(a)** The cruel soldiers praised the brave inhabitants. (5)

(b) The bold leader led the noble king back across the mountains. (7)

(c) He had not given food to the sad maidservant. (5)

(d) Few women loved the cruel leader. (5)

(e) All the farmers had wanted to build a huge temple. (6)

6.4 **(a)** fortes. (1)

(b) Subject: **dux**. Object: **regem**. (2)

(c) **tristis** is a 3rd declension adjective, and the dative singular ending does not rhyme with the dative singular ending of **ancilla**, which is a 1st declension noun. (1)

(d) 1st/2nd declension, like bonus. (1)

(e) Accusative singular neuter. (2)

Total marks: 35

6.5 **(a)** He was the bravest of all the Greeks. (2)

(b) Before Troy. (1)

(c) He was remaining there. (1)

(d) He was angry. (1)

(e) She was a girl who was very dear to Achilles, but Agamemnon had taken her away. (2)

(f) He was king. (1)

6.6 Achilles, who was the bravest of all the Greeks who were fighting before Troy, remained angrily in the camp. For the girl Briseis was very dear to the leader, but King Agamemnon had stolen the girl. 'I shall no longer fight,' he said, 'and I shall punish the cruel king. For the Greeks will not conquer the Trojans without me.' (20)

6.7 (a) (i) **fortissimus** or **carissima**. (1)

        (ii) **pugnabo**, **puniam** or **vincent**. (1)

    (b) Dative singular. **dux**. (2)

    (c) 1st person singular, future tense of **punio**. **punivit**. (3)

    (d) They will conquer. If someone is invincible, they can not be conquered. (2)

    (e) (i) **puella bona pueros amat**. (4)

        (ii) **nautae agricolam fessum spectabant**. (4)

Total marks: 45

Chapter 7

7.1 (a) The king did not give me a present. (5)

    (b) The leader was walking with me in the temple. (4)

    (c) My father will give the best wine to you. (6)

    (d) Who will give shields and arrows to us? (5)

    (e) We quickly gave help to you. (5)

7.2 (a) Dative singular. **ego**. (2)

    (b) **dux**. (1)

    (c) Accusative neuter singular, superlative of **bonus**. The best. (3)

    (d) Dative plural. Because it means *to us*. (2)

    (e) Nominative plural. Dative plural. (2)

Total marks: 35

7.3 (a) This boy loves that girl. (5)

    (b) The cruel king has punished this slave. (5)

    (c) The poet loved the girl; he used to give her many gifts. (7)

    (d) The father called his son and greeted him. (6)

    (e) The leader suddenly took that sword and wounded himself. (7)

7.4 (a) **hic** or **illam**. (1)

    (b) Masculine. (1)

    (c) The girl. (1)

    (d) The son. (1)

    (e) Reflexive. (1)

Total marks: 35

7.5 (a) Because the Trojans were now overcoming the Greeks in battle. (2)

    (b) To send messengers to Achilles. (2)

    (c) Achilles' companion. (1)

(d) They hurried to Achilles and Patroclus and ordered them to return to battle. (2)

(e) He said they would attack the enemy on their own, and that he would not return to fight unless the king returned his girl. (3)

7.6 Agamemnon was worried, because the Trojans were now overcoming the Greeks in battle. He therefore decided to send messengers to Achilles. The messengers hurried to Achilles and Patroclus, his companion, and ordered them to return to the battle. Achilles however said these words to the messengers: 'You will attack the forces of the enemy alone. I shall never return, unless the king hands over the girl to me. I now order you to go away.' (20)

7.7 (a) **mittere** = to send; **redire** = to return; **discedere** = to depart. (6)

(b) Genitive singular. **is, ea, id.** (2)

(c) Accusative plural. **haec.** (2)

(d) **oppugnavistis.** (1)

(e) Future. Trade, from **trado** = I hand over, is the process of *handing over* goods in exchange for money or other goods. (2)

(f) (i) **pueri laeti ancillas spectant.** (4)

(ii) **librum longum legebamus.** (3)

Total marks: 50

Chapter 8

8.1 (a) The Romans were not able to conquer the enemy. (4)

(b) The Greeks are not able to overcome the Trojans without the help of the gods. (7)

(c) The soldiers returned across the mountains into their native land. (5)

(d) The maidservants will go into the temple with the master. (4)

(e) The inhabitants had not been able to escape from the town. (4)

8.2 (a) 3rd person plural, imperfect tense of **possum. poterunt.** (3)

(b) **superare** = to overcome. (2)

(c) Accusative plural, because it follows **trans** (+ acc.) (2)

(d) **ineo. inire.** (2)

(e) Pluperfect. **poterit.** (2)

Total marks: 35

8.3 (a) You do love the three sons, don't you? (4)

(b) You are not carrying on the war against the enemy, are you? (5)

(c) We were not able to see the four temples. (4)

(d) Fifteen soldiers were fighting with eighteen farmers. (6)

(e) Surely you are able to see the six mountains and seven walls? (6)

Total marks: 25

8.4 (a) His Greek companions. (2)

(b) They wandered across the sea. (2)

(c) Very difficult. (2)

(d) Because the gods did not love them. (2)

(e) A beautiful island. (2)

(f) Ulysses immediately decided to look for food and water. (5)

8.5 Ulysses therefore divided his companions into two parts. He ordered most of the sailors to remain near the ship, but six sailors he ordered to search for food and water. These men soon came to a house. A very beautiful goddess, called Circe, lived in this house. When she saw the Greeks, she announced to them, 'I have food and wine. Surely you will come in, won't you, friends? Enter! I shall immediately prepare a very good dinner for you!' (30)

8.6 (a) (i) e Graecis or sine mora. (1)

(ii) timebant or esuriebant. (1)

(iii) intravit, constituit or intraverunt. (1)

(b) Man. Virile means manly, from **vir** = man. (3)

(c) Superlative adjective. Very wise. (2)

(d) Genitive singular, because it means *of* the goddess. (2)

(e) Perfect tense. **intrabant.** (2)

(f) (i) agricolae murum altum aedificant. (4)

(ii) puellae laetae feminas spectabant. (4)

Total marks: 65

Chapter 9

9.1 (a) The storm is greatly feared by all the sailors. (5)

(b) The courage of the soldiers is praised by the chief. (4)

(c) The old men and small boys are killed by the cruel guards. (5)

(d) The food and wine are prepared by the maidservants. (4)

(e) We are praised by the races of Greece, aren't we? (5)

9.2 (a) **tempestas.** (1)

(b) Genitive plural, because it means *of* the soldiers. (2)

(c) 3rd person plural, present passive of **occido. occidunt.** (3)

(d) 3rd person plural, present passive of **paro. paratur.** (3)

(e) 1st person plural, present passive of **laudo. laudate.** (3)

Total marks: 35

9.3 (a) A great reward was being given to the best leader by the king. (6)

(b) Meanwhile the guards were being slowly punished by the cruel chief. (6)

(c) The work will be done by the maidservants, won't it? (4)

(d) The animals will not be driven out of the fields, will they? (4)

(e) Yesterday the spears of the enemy and the weapons of the Romans were being collected by the guards. (7)

9.4 (a) 3rd person singular, imperfect passive of **do**. (2)

    (b) Ablative singular, because it agrees with **principe**. (2)

    (c) Future passive. **gerebatur**. (2)

    (d) **animalia**. (1)

    (e) **colligunt**. (1)

Total marks: 35

9.5 (a) Ten years. (1)

    (b) They destroyed it. (1)

    (c) Return to Greece and see their families and friends again. (3)

    (d) Wander across the sea. (2)

    (e) It was driven by a storm. (2)

    (f) The guard of the winds. (1)

9.6 When Troy, after ten years, had been captured, Ulysses and his Greek companions destroyed the city. Then they very much wanted to return to Greece and see their families and friends again. They wandered across the sea for a long time. At last their ship was driven by a storm to an island called Aeolia. This island was ruled by Aeolus, the guard of the winds. (20)

9.7 (a) Nominative plural. The addition of **-que** means 'and': and the companions. (2)

    (b) Perfect passive. **capio. cepit**. (3)

    (c) (i) **regebatur**. (1)

       (ii) **haec**. (1)

       (iii) Any of: **nomine, tempestate, custode**. (1)

    (d) 3rd person singular, perfect passive of **pello. pellere**.

       Repulsion is when something is driven away, from **repello =** I drive away. (4)

    (e) (i) **milites in urbem currebant**. (4)

       (ii) **omnes agricolae iuvenem laudabant**. (4)

Total marks: 50

Chapter 10

10.1 (a) The king who was attacking the city was feared by the citizens. (6)

    (b) All the citizens feared the king who was attacking the city. (7)

    (c) The island was ruled by a god who was the guard of the winds. (7)

    (d) All the affairs of the city, which the soldiers were defending, were managed by the citizens. (8)

    (e) The temple in which the poet was singing had been built by the inhabitants. (7)

10.2 (a) **rex**. Masculine. (2)

    (b) Accusative singular. It is the object of **oppugnabat**. (2)

    (c) Nominative, masculine, singular. (2)

(d) quam. Which. (2)

(e) Ablative neuter singular. It is in the ablative because it follows
in (+ abl.) = in. (2)

Total marks: 45

10.3 (a) Hope was given to the citizens by the chief himself. (5)

(b) Once the queen herself praised the faith of the inhabitants. (6)

(c) The soldiers themselves do not fear the weapons of the enemy. (6)

(d) The leader himself gave food and water to his soldiers. (7)

(e) You were not being guarded for a long time by the king himself,
were you? (6)

10.4 (a) principe. (1)

(b) Nominative, feminine, singular, because it agrees with **regina**, the
subject. (3)

(c) milites. Themselves. (2)

(d) Dative plural, because it agrees with **militibus**: to his soldiers. (2)

(e) Nominative plural. Because **vos** is the subject. (2)

Total marks: 40

10.5 (a) Well. (1)

(b) Brave. (1)

(c) A bag. (1)

(d) It contained all the winds. (2)

(e) They were hurrying to return to the ships. (3)

(f) He warned them not to try to open the bag. (3)

10.6 The Greeks were well received by King Aeolus. The king himself
wanted to give help to the brave Greeks and immediately handed
over to Ulysses a bag in which all the winds had been placed. Then
he said these words to him: 'Take this bag. With the help of these
winds you will be able to come safely to your fatherland.' Ulysses
therefore quickly warned his companions, who were hurrying to
return to the ships. 'Do not try to open this bag,' he said. (20)

10.7 (a) Nominative singular; **rex**. (2)

(b) (i) accepti sunt. (1)

(ii) quem or qui. (1)

(iii) Any of: bene, statim, tum, igitur, celeriter. (1)

(c) venti. Position comes from the PPP of **pono**, I place or position. (2)

(d) hic = this. (2)

(e) monebat. He warned. (2)

(f) (i) agricolae in templum cucurrerunt. (4)

(ii) duces cives fortes laudabant. (4)

Total marks: 50

Chapter 11

11.1 (a) The woman saw the old man carrying food. (5)

(b) The poet lived for a long time in the city, writing books. (6)

(c) The Romans were always feared by the citizens when they were waging war. (6)

(d) We made many journeys into the mountains, seeking gold. (6)

(e) The angry queen caught sight of the leader drinking wine in the temple. (7)

11.2 (a) Accusative masculine singular, present participle of **porto**. (2)

(b) Nominative masculine singular. (2)

(c) **gero. gerere**. (2)

(d) Subject: We. Object: **itinera**. (2)

(e) Imbibe means to drink, from the Latin **bibo** = I drink. **bibentes**. (2)

Total marks: 40

11.3 (a) They did not want to kill the leader who had been captured in war. (5)

(b) The farmer did not wish to frighten the animals which had been led into the field. (6)

(c) Who wants to eat the food prepared by the maidservants? (6)

(d) You will want to give arrows, collected by the inhabitants, to our soldiers, won't you? (8)

(e) The chief himself wanted to help the nine soldiers (who had been) driven out of their fatherland. (8)

11.4 (a) Accusative, masculine, singular of the past participle passive of **capio**. (2)

(b) Neuter. (1)

(c) **volo. velle**. (2)

(d) **sagittas**. (1)

(e) Volition means wishing, from **volo** = I wish. (1)

Total marks: 40

11.5 (a) He was a very famous Trojan leader. (2)

(b) Their city was destroyed by the Greeks. (2)

(c) A safe place. (2)

(d) Build a new city. (2)

(e) For many days. (2)

(f) Drive the Trojans out of his country. (2)

11.6 Aeneas was a very famous Trojan leader. When his city was destroyed by the Greeks, Aeneas fled from Troy with his friends. They sailed for a long time, looking for a safe place. At last they came to Italy, where they wanted to build a new city. For many days they were very happy there. But Turnus, who was the king of the Rutulians, a very savage race, wanted to drive the Trojans out of the land. (20)

11.7 (a) (i) Any of: **clarissimus, laetissimi, saevissimae.** (1)

(ii) **petentes.** (1)

(iii) **qui.** (1)

(b) Perfect passive. **deleo.** (2)

(c) Ablative singular; because it means *from* Troy. (2)

(d) 3rd person plural, imperfect tense of **volo.** (2)

(e) Accusative plural, because it is expressing time 'how long': for many days. (2)

(f) Present infinitive. To expel is to drive out, from **expello** = I drive out. (2)

Total marks: 45

Chapter 12

12.1 (a) We immediately ran to the river to find water. (6)

(b) We were attacking the city with spears and arrows in order to frighten the citizens. (7)

(c) All the farmers hurried into the fields to build a high wall. (7)

(d) The terrified inhabitants, freed by the soldiers, fled from Rome to save themselves. (8)

(e) The farmer drove the horse from the sea so as not to frighten it. (7)

12.2 (a) 1st person plural, imperfect subjunctive active of **invenio.** (2)

(b) Accusative plural, because it is the object of **terreremus.** (2)

(c) **aedifico. aedificare.** (2)

(d) **incolae.** Masculine. (2)

(e) Subjunctive. It is following **ne** + subjunctive in a purpose (final) clause. (2)

Total marks: 45

12.3 (a) The master often asked the slaves to prepare food. (6)

(b) The Roman leader ordered the soldiers to cross the river. (7)

(c) Yesterday with wise words the king persuaded the sailors to defend the ships bravely. (9)

(d) The soldier who had been captured by the enemy warned the citizens to flee from the town. (7)

(e) Surely you did not persuade the boys to run into the river? (6)

12.4 (a) It is subjunctive, following **ut** + subjunctive in a purpose (final) clause. (2)

(b) Dative plural. It is the indirect object of **imperavit.** (2)

(c) Ablative plural. It agrees with **verbis**, and means with wise words. (2)

(d) Nominative, masculine, singular of the past participle passive. **capere.** (2)

(e) 2nd person singular, perfect tense active of **persuadeo.** Persuasive means able to persuade, from **persuadeo** = I persuade. (2)

Total marks: 45

12.5 (a) They sailed. (1)

(b) To free Helen. (1)

(c) The island of Lemnos. (2)

(d) As a very famous leader. (2)

(e) Because he had been wounded by a snake. (2)

(f) For nine years. (2)

(g) He could not walk. (2)

(h) He had given him a bow, with which he killed animals. (3)

12.6 In the tenth year of the war, the Greeks were still fighting bravely, but were not able to destroy the walls or capture the city. At last Calchas, a very wise Greek prophet, said, 'You will never capture Troy except with the help of Philoctetes.' Therefore the Greeks sent messengers to immediately bring back Philoctetes, who had been left wounded on an island by his friends. They ordered them also to capture his bow. (30)

12.7 (a) (i) Any of: **advenerunt, invenerunt, persuasit, navigaverunt.** (1)

(ii) Any of: **navigare, vivere, redire.** (1)

(iii) **is** or **ei.** (1)

(b) They found. An invention is something that has been found out, from the Latin **invenio** = I find. (3)

(c) **ducem.** (1)

(d) Subject: **is.** Object: **duces Graecos.** (2)

(e) Ablative singular. By trickery. (2)

(f) **laetus navigavit.** (2)

(g) (i) **cum comitibus festinant.** (3)

(ii) **milites puellam fortem audiverunt.** (4)

Total marks: 65

Exam-style questions 13.1–16.1

Full answers are not given to these questions as the variety of possible answers is too great. Please refer to *Greeks and Romans* by A.M. Wright for more details.

Chapter 13

13.1 (a) Answers will depend on the adventures chosen. (10)

(b) See section 13.2. (10)

Chapter 14

14.1 (a) (i) See section 14.10. (8)

(ii) Exercise, socialising, cleanliness, business. (2)

(b) (i) See section 14.1. (8)

(ii) Any sensible answer would be acceptable here. Roman religion embraced a wide range of stories of gods interacting with mortals, and the divide between history, religion and mythology was blurred. (2)

Chapter 15

15.1 (a) (i) Roman dining rooms (*triclinia*) were arranged with three *lecti* (couches) for the diners to recline on. Food would be brought to the diners by slaves and placed on a table between the three couches. (8)

(ii) Eating lying down; no fork (2)

(b) (i) Slaves were put on display on a platform by slave dealers called *mangones* or *venalicii*. These markets would have been busy, noisy, crowded affairs, with potential purchasers shouting out prices or just commenting on the slaves on show. The slaves would have had a *titulus* (bill of sale) around their necks, advertising their personal qualities. (8)

(ii) Strength – to carry out hard work effectively.

Honesty – that they would not to steal from or defraud the master.

Good looks – to adorn the master's dinner parties.

Cooking skills – to help in the kitchen.

Numeracy – to help with the master's accounts. (2)

Chapter 16

16.1 (a) (i) See section 16.6. (8)

(ii) He might have lived in peace in Rome with his family; or he might have returned safely to Britain. (2)

(b) (i) Roman camps were rectangular, surrounded by a ditch (*fossa*) and a rampart (*agger*), with a wooden palisade on top of the rampart. They were laid out on a uniform grid system, with straight roads leading in through gates on each of the four sides. The camp would contain the *principia* (headquarters), *praetorium* (commander's quarters), *quaestorium* (paymaster's quarters), *basilica* (hall), a treasury and a *tribunal* (speaker's platform). There might also be a granary and a hospital. Permanent camps even contained *thermae* (baths) and a temple. (8)

(ii) To allow the soldiers to build the camps easily, following a well-rehearsed formula.

To allow soldiers to find their way around the camp, wherever it was. (2)

Test yourself answers

Chapter 1

1 capere.

2 Nominative.

3 Accusative.

4 veniunt.

5 Genitive plural. Of the words.

Chapter 2

1 They agree with (i.e. match) those of the noun.

2 est; sumus.

3 Accusative.

4 Ablative.

5 in (+ acc.) = into; in (+ abl.) = in.

Chapter 3

1 eram, eras, erat, eramus, eratis, erant.

2 intrabat, ridebat, bibebat, veniebat, iaciebat.

3 For emphasis.

4 Following prepositions that govern the accusative case; and when the pronoun is the object.

5 Adverbs, prepositions, conjunctions.

Chapter 4

1 3rd, they were running.

   1st, we were calling.

   3rd, you run.

   3rd, they have written.

   3½, he has made/done.

2 1st, of the spears.

   2nd, the walls.

   1st, the street.

   2nd, food.

   2nd, the dangers.

3 clamo, clamare, clamavi, clamatum = I shout.

video, videre, vidi, visum = I see.

mitto, mittere, misi, missum = I send.

venio, venire, veni, ventum = I come.

iacio, iacere, ieci, iactum = I throw.

4 unus, duo, tres, quattuor, quinque, sex, septem, octo, novem, decem.

5 secundus, quintus, decimus.

Chapter 5

1 dux, dux, ducem, ducis, duci, duce.

2 custodes, custodes, custodes, custodum, custodibus, custodibus.

3 corpus, corpus, corpus, corporis, corpori, corpore.

4 vulnera, vulnera, vulnera, vulnerum, vulneribus, vulneribus.

5 movebo, movebis, movebit, movebimus, movebitis, movebunt.

cadam, cades, cadet, cademus, cadetis, cadent.

faciam, facies, faciet, faciemus, facietis, facient.

Chapter 6

1 dormiveram, dormiveras, dormiverat, dormiveramus, dormiveratis, dormiverant.

2

crudelis	crudelis	crudele
crudelis	crudelis	crudele
crudelem	crudelem	crudele
crudelis	crudelis	crudelis
crudeli	crudeli	crudeli
crudeli	crudeli	crudeli

3

sapientes	sapientes	sapientia
sapientes	sapientes	sapientia
sapientes	sapientes	sapientia
sapientium	sapientium	sapientium
sapientibus	sapientibus	sapientibus
sapientibus	sapientibus	sapientibus

4 notior, notissimus.

sacrior, sacerrimus.

audacior, audacissimus.

facilior, facillimus.

5 melior, optimus.

minor, minimus.

peior, pessimus.

plus, plurimus.

Chapter 7

1 hic, hunc, huius, huic, hoc.

2 eae, eas, earum, eis, eis.

3 illud, illud, illius, illi, illo.

4 nolite ambulare!

5 puella se non vulnerabit.

Chapter 8

1 possum, potes, potest, possumus, potestis, possunt.

2 ibo, ibis, ibit, ibimus, ibitis, ibunt.

3 nonne?

4 num?

5 Any four of: adeo, exeo, ineo, pereo, transeo.

Chapter 9

1 factus.

2 videbitur.

3 rectus est.

4 vicerunt.

5 The 4th.

Chapter 10

1 The noun to which a relative pronoun refers.

2 quem.

3 ipsas.

4 eorundem.

5 Immediately after you have translated the antecedent.

Chapter 11

1 Like ingens.

2 Like bonus.

3 Using the accusative case.

4 Using the ablative case.

5 With the names of towns and small islands.

Chapter 12

1 ut/ne + subjunctive.

2 ut/ne + subjunctive. After **iubeo** and **cogo**, we use a present infinitive.

3 **essem, esses, esset, essemus, essetis, essent.**

4 **centum.**

5 **mille.**

Chapter 13

1 Daughter of Acrisius, mother of Perseus.

2 King of Colchis, father of Medea.

3 Minos.

4 Augeas.

5 Circe.

Chapter 14

1 Rhea Silvia.

2 He burnt his right hand in the fire, and thus became known as 'left-handed'.

3 Veturia.

4 The *scaena*.

5 The *apodyterium*.

Chapter 15

1 *Culina, triclinium, cubiculum, latrina.*

2 A *tunica laticlavia.*

3 *Cena.*

4 A slave who had been given his freedom.

5 The ferryman who transported the souls of the dead to the Underworld.

Chapter 16

1 Around 5300 men.

2 55 BC.

3 43 AD.

4 The Iceni.

5 117 km.